To Rabbi Wolpe,
An inspiration!
I hope you will
enjoy my dad's
story.

Respectfully,
Tanya

"All the Best!"

The Life *of* Victor M. Carter

by

Dr. Fanya Carter

Printed in the United States of America

First printed August 2007
in association with Hardscratch Press

ISBN: 978-0-9678989-8-8

TO MY HUSBAND JACK,
my mentor, my constant companion,
my best friend.

Contents

Author's Note

Thanks to the following individuals for their time and wisdom: Jeremy Berg, Shirley Carter, Rivian Chaikin, Herb Gelfand, Fanya Soll, Hugh Sommers, Esq., Edna Weiss, Evelyn Sterud, Roger Heimerl, and the Book Group: Pearl and Jack Berman, Lee and Fred Silton, Marion and Matt Solomon.

For their help in producing this book, I would like to thank Jackie Pels, David Johnson, Peter Kupfer and my cousin Susan Moore at Inkworks Press in Berkeley. Thanks also to Michael Levin for invaluable help with the initial preparation.

I also credit as resources for this work the two books by my grandfather Mark Carter, *The Russian Revolution As I Saw It* (Wolfer Printing, Los Angeles, 1959) and *"Okay America"* (Delmar Publishing, Los Angeles, 1963). Thanks to the *Wave* for permission to reprint in its entirety my father's obituary.

Finally, I wish to acknowledge Internet Movie Database (IMDb) as a source for material about Republic Pictures and Herbert Yates.

About the Title

MY FATHER HAD A FAVORITE EXPRESSION for greeting people and saying good-bye: "All the Best!" He derived the phrase from the Israeli expression he loved, *"Kal tu'uv,"* which could also be translated as "All good things." I can still see my father giving, wishing, doing, and receiving all the best that life had to offer. He truly personified the phrase "All the Best," the most appropriate title for the remarkable story of his life.

Family Tree
(abridged)

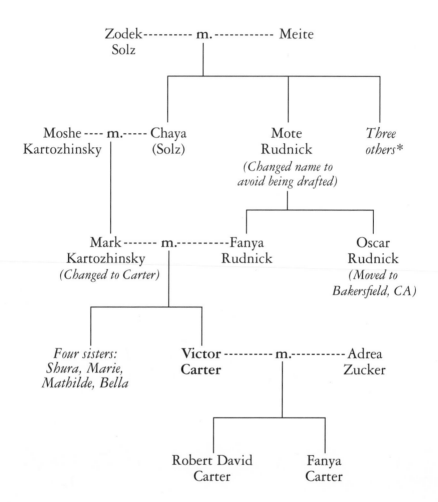

Zodek Solz --------- m. ------------ Meite

Moshe ---- m. ----- Chaya (Solz)
Kartozhinsky

Mote Rudnick
(Changed name to avoid being drafted)

*Three others**

Mark ------- m. ----------Fanya Rudnick
Kartozhinsky
(Changed to Carter)

Oscar Rudnick
(Moved to Bakersfield, CA)

Four sisters: Shura, Marie, Mathilde, Bella

Victor Carter ---------- m. ----------- Adrea Zucker

Robert David Carter

Fanya Carter

*Isaac Solz Schmuilovich, a *shochet*, or kosher butcher, moved to Siberia; Schleime, born in Lubitsch, lived his entire life there; Schprintze Solz Woolfovich, name changed to Wolf. The Wolf family lives in England.

1

Meet Victor Carter

IT IS HARDLY AN EXAGGERATION to say that my father, Victor Carter (Kartozhinsky), was born in a hail of bullets. He spent the early years of his childhood in prerevolutionary Russia, a time of intense political intrigue and constant violence and bloodshed. It took the "Carter luck" to survive those turbulent years. He was born in 1909, between the revolutionary uprisings in 1905 and 1917.

When I was a little girl, my father told me stories of the military police forcing him to identify the corpses of people who lay dead in the streets outside his family's home. The soldiers, who were illiterate, would take the wallets from the people they had just killed and bring them to my father, so that he could read them the victims' names from their identification papers.

And yet, from this traumatic and terrifying childhood, a man would emerge who would transform the world for millions of people in our country and across the globe.

The Kartozhinsky family immigrated to the United States in 1921, when my father was twelve. He passed away in 2004 at the age of ninety-four. In his lifetime, he helped build the family business, Carter Hardware in downtown Los Angeles, into one of the most successful and innovative retail stores in the nation. He then left the business and took what he later called his "first retirement," after which he created a hugely successful manufacturing business, Vimcar. This business served as a springboard to even greater business success as a supplier to the U.S. government during World War II. When the war ended, my father followed his instinct for recognizing change. He used his acumen in the hardware business to develop Builders Emporium, initially a tiny hardware store, into the largest and most successful hardware and home store of its era, comparable today to The Home Depot. The location was the San Fernando Valley, just north of Los Angeles, home to thousands of returning GIs and their young families.

When he sensed that he had taken that business as far as he could, my father sold it and began another sabbatical. He weighed his options and several years later bought a controlling interest in Republic Pictures, a then-struggling movie studio specializing in turning out B movies that invariably starred the wife of the studio owner. My father recognized, long before most others did, the potential of television, and he turned Republic Studios into a highly innovative—and highly profitable—center of television production. He also recognized the value inherent in the fact that Republic's stock was traded on the New York Stock Exchange, and transformed the business into a holding company for large national concerns. In less than a decade under my father's direction, the company increased in value by more than ten times.

My father's life was certainly about business, but it would be grossly inaccurate to suggest that it was only about business. He and my mother celebrated more than seventy-five years of love, affection, and devotion. My father never lost sight of the importance of his marriage, and he never let success turn his head or cause him to value his wife or family any less. He epitomized the Yiddish term *menschlichkeit*, defined as "a subtle mixture of intelligence, wisdom, and compassion."

My parents, Victor and Adrea, had two children, my brother Robert David and me. Robert passed away in his teens as a result of muscular dystrophy. This was the one personal challenge that all of my father's energy, intelligence, and determination could not overcome, and it was the chief tragedy of his life.

The loss of his son, combined with the intense memories of anti-Semitism and despotism from his childhood in Russia, affected my father deeply. It drove him to contribute his great wealth, his intelligence, his ideas, and his extraordinary capacity for making things happen to a breathtakingly wide variety of social, medical, educational, and religious causes, in the United States and around the world.

My father was a major donor and advisor to the highest levels of the Israeli government and business leadership. In those roles, he was instrumental in the formation of the State of Israel in 1948 and in that country's economic and political survival in the ensuing decades. Throughout his later life he kept a home in Jerusalem overlooking the Old City. His philanthropy extended to Israel's social welfare, its cultural institutions, its hospitals, its universities, and its parks. He served on the board of Hebrew University in Jerusalem and was founder and chairman of the American Friends of Tel Aviv University. My father also donated a collection of Jewish art that he had acquired from Scholem Asch, the great Yiddish writer and dramatist, to the Israel Museum in Jerusalem. A great lover of music, he helped to found the Tel Aviv University Philharmonic Orchestra.

Closer to home, my father was deeply involved in the civil rights movement. He played leadership roles in the Urban League and the NAACP. He was a close friend of Dr. Martin Luther King Jr. As an appointee to the Los Angeles Fire Commission, one of countless public service positions my father held over the course of his long lifetime, he was personally responsible for the racial integration of the Los Angeles Fire Department.

He was instrumental in bringing about the desegregation of the Los Angeles Unified School District and ending housing discrimination in Crenshaw, Compton, and Inglewood, mixed-race neighborhoods in and around Los Angeles. He eased the tensions between the city's police and its black residents by seeing to the appointment of the city's first black police commissioner. He was also instrumental in the election of his dear friend Tom Bradley to the mayoralty of Los Angeles. Bradley became the first black mayor in the city's history and one of the first black mayors of any major American city. At my father's passing, a leading black newspaper in Southern California, the *Wave*, eulogized him as "a giant in the black community."

The list of his civic and cultural involvements in Los Angeles is remarkable in its length and diversity. The Greater Los Angeles United Way, for which he served as president, celebrated his record of civic accomplishment by creating the Victor M. Carter Humanitarian Award. He was deeply involved with the Jewish community as president of the Jewish Federation Council of Greater Los Angeles. He established three architecture scholarships at the University of Southern California.

My father's business and cultural interests spanned the Pacific as well. In the 1920s and '30s, my father came to know many Japanese-Americans, including customers of his family's Carter Hardware store in downtown Los Angeles and owners of neighboring businesses. His interest in Japanese business and culture drew him to visit Japan in 1937, one of the most enjoyable trips he ever took. The December 1941 attack on Pearl Harbor came as a huge shock to my father, as it did to the rest of the country. He fought bitterly against the internment of Japanese-Americans during the war, many of whose homes and businesses were taken from them and never returned. My father never forgot the fundamental unfairness of that act and kept a photograph of a Japanese internment camp on his desk at work, even into the 1980s. I once asked him why he kept that photo within view. He said, "I never want to forget the wrong that was done to these people."

He often would tell me that the Japanese-Americans who had been living in America for decades prior to the war had no responsibility for the actions of Emperor Hirohito, and that our country ought to have been ashamed of the way it treated its citizens of Japanese extraction. His efforts on behalf of Japanese-Americans, including his work to help establish the first Japanese-American bank in the United States after World War II, led to his becoming president of the Japan-America Society of Southern California.

My father's interests went beyond business, philanthropy and community. He was the ultimate "people person." He loved to spend time with beloved friends, family, and business associates. He had the gift for making everyone in the room feel fascinating, important, and in the case of the ladies, beautiful. My father remained faithful to his wedding vows, and yet he deeply enjoyed the presence of women. He was extremely generous with his compliments, especially for those who were not the most beautiful. Indeed, the less attractive the woman, the more likely my father was to tell her, "You look more beautiful than ever tonight!"

If you visited a restaurant with my father, it would take fifteen minutes from the time he stood up to leave until he reached the front door. There were lots of hands to shake, smiles and stories to exchange, and love and good cheer to share with acquaintances from business, philanthropy, the sports and entertainment worlds, and from every walk of life in Los Angeles.

My father was a friend and trusted advisor to mayors, governors, presidents, and Israeli prime ministers, and to the workingman as well. I will never forget that at my father's funeral a detachment of the Los Angeles Fire Department appeared, to pay its final farewell to a man who had been so instrumental in bringing it into the modern world.

I recall as a child how beloved my father was in the community. His wisdom was so sought after that people would literally circle the block on Sundays, so that they could have a few minutes with Victor Carter. They would ask him to resolve a business matter, offer guidance in a family dispute, or otherwise smooth the turbulent waters of personal lives. Approached with a personal question, he would always say, "Come over to my house on Sunday, and we can talk about it then." Myriads of people took him up on that invitation over the years, and on Sunday afternoons and even into the evenings, my father belonged to those who sought and received the benefit of his extraordinary experience and broad wisdom.

I admired my father's success in business, philanthropy, and civic affairs, and the friendships he made and kept for decades. I deeply appreciated him because of the extraordinary warmth he showered upon me—from my earliest childhood through the turbulent years of adolescence and all the way through adulthood.

On Sunday mornings when I was a child, my father belonged to me. I would make him loosely scrambled eggs, and lightly browned toast, just the way he liked it. He would tell me stories of his childhood and the Russian Revolution, the family's sudden escape from Russia, and tales of survival in Constantinople, as the Carter family struggled on their journey to America.

My father gave me so much. He gave me the confidence to know that I could accomplish anything I wished. He made me feel beautiful, even when I didn't feel that way. In short, my father gave me ... me. On occasion, the toughness he displayed in the business world would intrude into our relationship. However, the overwhelming majority of our time together was an intense experience of mutual appreciation. It reflected the love of his mother as well as the feelings he had for his wife, my mother, Adrea. His story is of a man who succeeded at nearly everything in life, with the painful exception, of course, of his battle to save his son from muscular dystrophy. In every other way, my father was a huge success, a giant among men. And above all, he was my daddy.

The purpose of this book is to create a monument to his life. I want to share the love, the wisdom, and the magnificence of his life with you, as well as share the story of an intense, extraordinary friendship and bond between a father and daughter that lasted for more than seventy years. This is my father's story ... and ours.

Victor's paternal grandparents, Moshe and Chaya Kartozhinsky.

The Kartozhinsky family in Russia, c. 1917: Victor, Shura, Mathilde and Marie, with their mother, Fanya. Youngest sister Bella was not yet born.

The Carter (Kartozhinsky) family in the United States, 1927: back row, left to right, Maurice and Shura (Carter) Kompaniez, Mathilde, Marie and Victor; front row, Mark, Bella and Fanya.

A lesson from Mom.

Cousins Victor and Willie Carter—young cut-ups.

2

A Russian Soul

MY FATHER TOLD ME THE SAME STORIES over and over again. He told me of recurring dreams that he was being chased, a dream that surely grew from his memories of Russia. Today, as a therapist with more than thirty-five years of practice, I look back on those moments of a father sharing his stories and dreams with his little girl. I can interpret my father's need to tell and retell those stories, especially the experience of identifying the dead bodies for the Russian military police, as a manifestation of what we today call post-traumatic stress syndrome. He needed to tell me those stories and he could talk easily to me. I was a willing and avid listener, because I treasured him—and his time and attention—so much. I was the enthusiastic recipient of his many stories. I was fascinated by the colorful, dramatic events from his childhood that he shared with me.

The best way to understand my father's lust for life, his drive for success, and his love of good times, fun and celebration, is to understand the Russian soul. My father was a deeply passionate individual who thoroughly engaged with life, deeply desirous of filling his every waking moment with accomplishment. I attribute that to his Russian upbringing.

When you think of nineteenth-century Russia, you think of the larger-than-life characters leaping from the pages of a Tolstoy novel, the passion of a Tchaikovsky piano concerto, and the humorous, soulful nature of Russian Jewish life captured in a painting by Marc Chagall. My father's character comprised all of these elements—passion, intelligence, an earthy sense of humor, and an innate desire to survive every obstacle that an uncaring world might throw in his path. My father was born between the twilight years of the czar and the bloody uprisings that presaged the Russian Revolution. For the Russian Jews of my father's childhood, life was an obstacle course. In late-nineteenth-century Russia, as in many places throughout Europe, Jews still lived in ghettos—walled-in, segregated areas closed to the business, cultural, and educational life of the surrounding city. For most Jews, opportunities for economic advancement were highly limited. The ghettos themselves were small, squalid, and subject to fire and disease. In many cities, Jews who left the ghetto during the day had to wear badges identifying their religion. They had to return at night to be locked into the ghetto or they would face criminal penalties.

For several generations, my father's family had been able to live outside the ghetto in Rostov-on-Don, because of an exception to the rule restricting Jews to the ghetto. If you were Jewish and you ran a business that employed five hundred or more individuals, you were free to live outside the ghetto. My great-grandfather Moshe Kartozhinsky, together with his father, built a business selling hardware and other implements for farmers. It is truly remarkable that Moshe's forebears, working with limited capital and in the highly anti-Semitic atmosphere in which they lived, were able to raise themselves from the ghetto and create the underpinnings of what became a large and highly successful business. The factory allowed Moshe and his wife, Chaya, to live in comfort and dignity outside the ghetto's walls. The factory wasn't just a means of earning a livelihood. It was a ticket to freedom.

Rostov-on-Don is in southeast Russia and remains a major port to this day. It was an important producer of farm equipment (an aspect of its history in which my family played a role) and a leading exporter of grain. The port of Rostov-on-Don moved huge amounts of grain every year, and the farmers who lived in the surrounding communities needed farming tools. So my great-grandfather Moshe built and enlarged the factory until it employed 500 workers, enabling him to make a good living and move his family to a better part of town.

A passageway connected the factory and the beautiful home Moshe built for his family. My great-grandmother Chaya had come to Russia from Lithuania; she ran the factory along with her sons and her daughter. Moshe and Chaya had five children— my grandfather Mark, my great-aunt Sonya, and my great-uncles George, Oscar, and Israel. My great-grandmother had an authoritative air. She ruled that factory and all who worked there. If she saw someone idling, she would not suffer that silently.

The factory contained a shop floor where the mechanical devices were manufactured, a business area where negotiations and deals took place, an office for Chaya, and a room where my great-grandfather would remain, deep in prayer, and from which he emerged every so often, to monitor the workmen and the deal-making. By modern standards, of course, the factory would appear to be a fairly primitive affair, because all of its activities were taking place practically one on top of the other. But an enterprise that employed five hundred people was substantial. Business acumen, therefore, was a family tradition that stretched back generations before my father was born.

One morning, when Moshe was coming to the factory, some typically anti-Semitic Russians grabbed him and shot him in the eye—for no reason other than the fact that he was Jewish. The shooting practically blinded him, and it took him many years to recover. After the shooting, he did not feel that he was as helpful in the factory as in the past. He had always been a highly religious person, and he now spent even more of his time in prayer. My father told me that he would frequently see my great-grandfather davening, praying, in a small room attached to the factory.

That shooting was typical of the violence of the era. Bullets flew, anti-Semitism was rampant, and my great-grandfather was lucky to have escaped with his life. My great-uncle Israel was arrested during this period and sent to Siberia. Unlike many less fortunate Jews, he survived the ordeal and returned. The world into which my father was born held constant and life-threatening dangers for Jews.

In the early 1900s, sons went into their fathers' businesses as a matter of course. It wasn't like today, where you go to college and then figure out what you're going to major in and then decide, eventually, what you want to do with your life. Back then, you went to work for your father. Additionally, in Russia at that time, it was nearly impossible for Jews to receive a university education, to find work in the professions, to own land and run a farm, or to enter the government. If your father or uncle had a business, therefore, it made economic sense to go to work for him. In the case of the Kartozhinsky factory, everybody worked in that family business. My great-grandparents Moshe and Chaya Kartozhinsky truly accomplished something remarkable by building and running that business.

Today, we think of the Russian Revolution as an episode in history that started in October 1917. In reality, numerous factions in Russia had been competing for years to rid the country of its brutal and hated czar. There were bloody uprisings in 1905 and 1917, years that bracketed my father's birth in 1909. One never knew from week to week which faction would be in charge—the Czarists, the revolution-minded Bolshevists, the more moderate Menshevists, or the more liberal Kerenskyites. One could be sure, however, that violence and murder would accompany every shift in the political winds.

The first two elements that shaped my father's character, therefore, were his family's business tradition and the dangerous times in which he grew up. The third element is his spirituality, which he expressed through his love of people. My great-grand-father Moshe and my grandfather Mark had a powerful religious upbringing in Russia. The men of the Kartozhinsky family attended cheder—religious school—and my great-grandfather and my grandfather attended religious services regularly.

My evidence for my grandfather Mark's religious training is the fact that when he came to America, he would lead the entire Passover seder in Hebrew with a fluency that can only be ac-quired in childhood. As a child, I was always struck by the great joy my grandfather took in leading the seder. I can still see him sitting at the head of the table, singing the songs with such joy and intensity, often with sixty guests seated around their vast, elegant dining room table. He wrote two books, his autobiogra-phy and his account of the Russian Revolution. In each, he told of attending religious services with his father. He also served as a member of the Jewish Community Council of the city of Ros-tov-on-Don.

My father was not especially interested in traditional reli-gious practice. I would define him as a man who was more spir-itual in nature than one who was committed to ritual. I don't know how much religious training he had received during his early youth in Russia, but once his family began its odyssey to the New World, he received little if any Jewish training at all. He was by nature a man of action. He lacked the patience for the kind of religious training and adherence to practice that tradi-tional Judaism requires. Instead, I see him as a deeply spiritual man, even though his spirituality did not evidence itself in terms of ritual and formal prayer.

My father's love for people—family members, friends, em-ployees and individuals who benefited by the scores of civic, charitable and cultural organizations he supported—was the means by which his spiritual nature revealed itself. He was not one to sit around and ponder the existence of God. My father was a doer, and his main religious practice was in terms of making life better for everyone around him.

He inherited his business sense and his intense desire to be his own man from his father. Yet when it came to personality, he was much more like his beloved mother, my namesake, Fanya. My grandmother Fanya came to Rostov-on-Don from Vilna. Back then, the Russians, especially the more successful Russian Jews living in Rostov-on-Don, thought of rural Vilna as a kind of "country bumpkin" land. Rostov-on-Don was a thriving business community. Because of its busy port, it was a transportation hub in that part of Russia. My grandmother came to that thriving metropolis from a farming community that the urban dwellers of Rostov looked on as somewhat beneath their dignity.

Fanya's father was a farmer and the brother of Chaya, Moshe's wife. Fanya was considered something of a poor relation coming to the big city. Why did Mark and Fanya marry, considering my grandfather's concern about class distinctions? It was most likely timing and attraction, the same factors that cause most people to marry. My grandmother Fanya was very attractive and very big-hearted, a generous, warm, caring human being, eager to help and please in whatever way she could. These qualities must have endeared her to Mark. And she was deeply attracted to him. She appreciated being a part of the family in Rostov-on-Don.

Fanya had no formal education but had wonderful skills with people. She was very charitable and always remained considerate and sensitive to the plight of the less fortunate. The marriage between Mark and Fanya succeeded because my grandmother was such a kind person. She adored him and happily did everything for him. She was a tireless worker on behalf of her marriage and family and anyone else for whom she cared deeply. She also contributed to many of my father's best traits—his earthy nature, his passion for life, his love of people, and his enjoyment of the simple pleasures of eating, drinking, laughing, and storytelling. My father embodied kindness and generosity, characteristics he inherited from his mother.

One of the most important moments in my father's childhood came when his mother took him on a trip to Odessa. There, they distributed many pairs of shoes to the children of that city's impoverished Jewish community. The words that my grandmother spoke to my father that day shaped his destiny: "You always have to give back. Make sure you're always giving back."

In sum, the dominant characteristics of my father's personality are legacies of his upbringing as a Russian Jew. I define these traits as his outsized love of life, his extraordinary business sense, his ability to develop and lead large enterprises, his spirituality, which evidenced itself not in terms of outward piety but in terms of love and commitment to his fellow man, and his disdain for people who took themselves too seriously. He was an amalgam of the spiritual, intellectual, and business heritage of the Kartozhinsky family of Rostov-on-Don and the compassion and big-heartedness his mother imbued in him. The soul of my father is a uniquely Russian Jewish soul, a soul as attuned to the needs of fellow human beings as it is to the subtleties of the business world.

As the terrors of revolutionary Russia unfolded, it became increasingly clear that leaving was a necessity if the family was to survive. Their journey to freedom begins in the next chapter.

3

Leaving Russia

MY FATHER'S EARLY CHILDHOOD IN RUSSIA was a time of enormous contradictions. The family lived in wealthy surroundings—in a beautiful, twelve-room, two-story home modeled on the English country-house style. Peter the Great opened the doors in Russia to European ideas in culture and design, and the wealthiest and most aristocratic families lived in homes built in keeping with design elements borrowed from Western Europe. Labor was inexpensive and the household employed numerous servants. My father had not one but several wet nurses—as an infant, he had all the milk he could possibly have desired!

Jews were not permitted to attend public school in Rostov-on-Don, so my father and his sisters had the benefit of private tutors who came to the home. My father enjoyed an active childhood and told me repeatedly of the pleasure he took from riding wild horses, Cossack-style. The household was a vibrant one, with a constant babble of voices. And with four high-spirited sisters, he could barely get a word in edgewise! His ever-present mother provided all the love and support the only boy among five children could need.

It was a complex time in Russia from a political standpoint, with the various parties jockeying, often violently, for position. My father often spoke of his experiences as a little boy walking the streets of Rostov-on-Don while bullets flew all around him. He may have lost some of his hearing due to the artillery rounds fired at close range as he made his way to and from the house. He would literally have to dodge bullets in order to get home.

As the Russian Revolution approached, the violence reached a crescendo. It became increasingly clear to Mark that his family could no longer remain in Russia. At the time, though, leaving Russia was no easy matter. The authorities rarely gave Jews permission to leave. Paradoxically, the very business that was the source of my family's success and financial well-being may have been the reason the Russian government would never have allowed them to leave. With five hundred employees, the factory was too important to be abandoned or shuttered. If the Kartozhinskys left Rostov-on-Don, what would happen to those five hundred families?

And even if the government gave permission to my father's family to depart Rostov-on-Don, where would they go? It was a crime to take money out of Russia, and the life of an immigrant passing through Europe, seeking transport to the United States, would not be easy. Furthermore, there were no guarantees that passage to the United States could be arranged.

In addition, there was the language barrier to consider. My father and his family spoke little or no English. In addition to Russian, they did have some fluency in German and French, the languages of the aristocracy that tutors taught my father and his sisters. So the situation in Rostov-on-Don, both for Jews in general and for the Kartozhinskys in particular, was extraordinarily serious. Staying could be life-threatening. Seeking to leave could result in deportation to Siberia or immediate execution.

The situation grew more dire. Two years after the Russian Revolution, in late December 1919, the Bolsheviks took over Rostov-on-Don. Mark noted in his autobiography that the weather that winter was especially brutal—often as cold as twenty-eight degrees below zero. Refugees and wounded soldiers swelled the population of the city from its usual 300,000 to 350,000 inhabitants to more than one million. Landlords gouged tenants while the Communists simply took over homes, factories, and offices. Soldiers were billeted in the

Kartozhinsky home. Across the street from their home, the G.P.U. or Central Police, the forerunner to the K.G.B., seized the home of a banker and used the basement as a torture chamber. Mark recalls in his memoirs the cries of men being beaten to death in that basement.

On Christmas Eve 1919, the Communists went on a killing spree. Mark told of dead bodies, frozen, hanging from trees, and expressed his disgust that the birthday of the Christian savior could be ignored in this manner. On another gruesome night, soldiers shot dead anyone who ventured outdoors. The next morning, Mark said, more than 1,500 naked bodies lay in the streets of Rostov-on-Don. He wrote of his fear that his son, Victor, would be traumatized for life by the spectacle. This was the occasion on which the soldiers, their hands literally dripping with blood, would bring the ten-year-old Victor the wallets of the people they had just killed, who still lay dead in the streets around their house, so that the boy could identify them. The soldiers were illiterate peasants who knew how to fire a gun and kill people but did not know how to read.

It was unbearable for my father to read the names of those deceased, many of whom were family friends, neighbors, customers, or employees of the business, individuals whom he saw killed in the streets by the soldiers who had taken over his home. He naturally obeyed the soldiers, because the consequences would have been fatal had he refused. At this point, factories like our family's had been nationalized, and Moshe and Mark lived in fear that they would be killed because they were bourgeois. Friends of Mark's were killed, exiled to Siberia, sent to work in coal mines (a certain death), or otherwise stripped of their fortune and dignity. By now it was clear—the family simply had to leave. If their home had been taken, how much longer would they control the factory anyway? And if the Bolsheviks were to be in charge for long, personal property, wealth, or other signposts of affluence would be stripped from them anyway. With the rise of the Bolsheviks, my family's days in Russia were dwindling.

But it was still illegal to depart. The dilemma was stark. Stay and lose everything, and risk meeting with a stray bullet or with the bullet from an executioner's weapon, or take one's chances and try to escape. Escape was the only practical alternative. But the problem remained: how to get a passport or travel documents without government permission, and with the risk that the G.P.U. would discover the family's plans to leave—and shoot them on the spot.

Justice in those early days of the Soviet revolution—if it can be called justice—consisted of quick trials, which in Rostov-on-Don took place in the home of a cousin of Mark's. Men would plead with the court for their lives, because practically anything could be construed as a capital crime against the state—owning property, employing a worker, withholding one's produce from marauding soldiers. Instead of declaring a death sentence, the court would say that it would continue its work the next day— a cue for a two-man death squad, armed with revolvers, to await the victim as he emerged from the "courthouse." The victim would be shot then and there.

Help arrived from a most unlikely source. A family maid, whom Mark describes as especially beautiful and who had always been close with the Kartozhinskys, was having an affair with one of the soldiers. She asked this soldier if he would help our family escape, and he agreed, in exchange for a reward. Mark and Fanya dug up diamonds and other jewels they had previously hidden away in the yard. Some of the jewels went to the soldier as compensation for his assistance. The rest of the precious stones were sewn into bedsheets so they could be smuggled out of the country. As the family made the dangerous journey out of Russia, across Europe, and to the United States and freedom, they would survive by selling the diamonds and jewels and by using them to bribe police, soldiers, or government officials.

In those times, a family of seven—five children and their parents—could not simply turn up at the train station at Rostov-on-Don. Even with whatever governmental assistance or permission that the family maid's soldier-boyfriend had been able to secure, leaving as a family was not an option. The Kartozhinskys would have to make their way to the railway station one by one.

On countless Sunday mornings, my father told me the story of his father, Mark, hiding in an underground "refrigerator" on the day they were to escape. In those days, a refrigerator was essentially a hole in the ground where families kept food cool and fresh. My grandfather hid there all night. According to my father, his father's hair turned white that night. When I knew him, he always had a full head of white hair. Mark wrote in his memoirs of hiding in such a crawl space under the house on two separate occasions, to avoid being killed by the soldiers or the police. On one of those occasions, he writes, mice crawled over his body, and on the other, the family dog stayed with him and had to be muzzled so as not to give his position away.

On the morning they were to leave, Mark told Victor and the other children, "Don't look left or right. Just hurry to the train station. Do not even think about saying good-bye to any of your friends—no one can know what we are attempting to do." The five children were instructed to go separately; had they gone as a group, they would have attracted attention and most likely been arrested. My father often told me how sad he felt that he never had a chance to say good-bye to his boyhood friends or relatives, and that he never saw any of them again. The secret preparations the family made in order to escape culminated with Mark spending the night in that refrigerator. No one could know what they planned to do.

My grandfather wrote that as the time neared for their departure, he tried to collect money from as many people as possible who had borrowed from him or who owed the business any money, to accumulate as much as possible for the trip. The day for their departure had arrived, and Mark recalled in his autobiography:

> I was overjoyed, yet frantic with worry that the Communists would see us leaving. I knew what the consequences would be. On the important day, I left the house as I usually did, with my briefcase. I took the streetcar and went to the depot. The family left separately in taxis or in different streetcars, and one of my former employees took all of our belongings in a truck. Now I felt we were really going. I had my identification given to me by our commissar, but still I did not want to be seen leaving the city. I sat in our rail car for hours, until our car from the freight lines was transferred to the main line passenger train. I wore a khaki shirt, pants, and a soldier's cap. In this manner, I sat for hours. It grew dark, and the light was bad. And I saw the secret police go through the train. Thank heaven, they did not question me. At 8:00 p.m., our train left for Tiflis. Destination—Freedom![1]

With diamonds sewn into their bedsheets, the Kartozhinsky family quietly converged at the train station—their beautiful

---

1. Carter, Mark, *The Russian Revolution As I Saw It*, p. 207

home, the business that had taken generations to build, family, friends, and business ties, all abandoned. No longer would they live the lives of aristocrats with servants, tutors, and wild horses for young Victor to ride. Fortunately, the authorities had not noticed them separately boarding that train. The childhoods of the five Kartozhinsky children ended abruptly as the train picked up speed and headed toward their next stop, the city of Tiflis in the Ukraine. As Mark wrote in his autobiography, their destination truly was freedom, but there would be nothing easy about that journey.

4

To America

THE TRAIN ON WHICH THE KARTOZHINSKY FAMILY had se-
cretly assembled itself traveled from Rostov-on-Don to the city
of Tiflis, now known as Tbilisi. The Russian Empire had occu-
pied Tiflis in the region of Georgia in 1801, and now the locale
offered safe haven for the family. They had to bribe their way
into the city, Mark wrote, and nearly faced deportation when the
local authorities declared Mark's passport fake. The family was
only able to receive official permission to enter Tiflis when Mark
promised to pay a most unusual bribe—he had to procure a cow
for the mistress of a leading government official, so she could
provide milk for her young daughter!

Mark had chosen Tiflis as a refuge for the family because it
was on the way to Western Europe and because he had a friend
there who had promised the family comfortable accommoda-
tions. Instead, he gave the entire family of seven a single room
in which to live. To make matters worse, Tiflis was also so rife
with anti-Semitism that my father could not attend public
school. The only good news was that they were safe from the
bullets flying in Rostov-on-Don.

Mark left his hometown because of the strong possibility
that he would have been tried and executed as a member of the
bourgeoisie. Of course, the Bolsheviks would never have given a
thought to the fact that my grandfather had provided a livelihood for five hundred families. Without our family's factory,
what would those individuals have done for work? The Bolsheviks would also have ignored the other contributions our family
made to the city: taxes, manufacturing abilities, and the commerce any large, successful enterprise generates.

Most likely, they would have stood Mark up against the wall as a "traitor to the workers," and shot him. Thus, as grim as it was, a single room in anti-Semitic Tiflis was far more desirable than living with the uncertainty and likely death that awaited had they remained in Rostov-on-Don.

The seven of them lived in that room for six months, waiting for the opportunity to go to Turkey, from which they could travel either to England or the United States. Constantinople, now Istanbul, located on the Bosphorus, is one of the central ports in Eastern Europe. From its harbor one could travel practically anywhere. During those six months in Tiflis, my grandparents were corresponding with cousins in England. They were considering immigrating to that country, but our cousins informed my grandparents that they were much better off going to America, because they thought the political situation there was better for Jews.

While in Tiflis, my grandmother contracted jaundice. This was another story my father told me. He had to keep searching the town for mineral water to aid her recovery. Mineral water was a luxury in revolution-era Tiflis, but even then, at the age of ten, my father had begun to demonstrate his resourcefulness, no matter how difficult the circumstances. For this reason, the family called him the *copsanayus*, a Russian military term equivalent to the English term quartermaster. This is the individual who goes ahead of his unit during the war and finds everything it needs in order to survive and fight. Victor was already the *copsanayus*.

The family had to remain in Tiflis until my grandmother became well enough to travel on to Constantinople. As my father had already abandoned school, he spent most of his days hunting for mineral water for her. Finally the time came for them to travel to Constantinople. They arrived in the port city on December 29, 1920, with the equivalent of $1.50 in cash to their names.

Constantinople was a considerable relief after Tiflis. The city was much larger and more cosmopolitan than Rostov-on-Don, but it possessed the kind of business-oriented locale with which my family was familiar. No one would have confused Rostov-on-Don with Constantinople, but the two cities were thriving business communities with busy ports. In some ways, it must have felt like home.

Another advantage of Turkey, compared with either Tiflis or Rostov-on-Don, was that anti-Semitism was less rampant. The Turks of Istanbul were far more tolerant of Jews than were the Russians. The new living situation was bearable, and soon the family would abandon Europe altogether to go to the United States. Their primary concern, aside from my grandmother's health, was financial. Their net worth was limited to the remaining jewels they had smuggled out of Rostov-on-Don, into and out of Tiflis, and into Constantinople. That wealth had already been seriously depleted by the cost of travel, living, and bribes that Mark had to dispense along the way. Fortunately, in Constantinople Mark received the equivalent of $1,500[1] from a local bank he had represented in Russia. That money allowed them to purchase tickets, seven months later, for their passage to New York.

I often think about the fragility of their financial position. What if they had not received that $1,500? If those bedsheets containing the jewels had been lost, stolen, or discovered by the authorities, they would have been penniless. At that, the family was at the mercy of the diamond dealers and jewelers they en-

---

1. Presumably the value in 1959 dollars, the year in which he wrote his memoirs.

countered en route, who knew exactly what they were dealing with—refugees whose life savings had been converted into precious stones, and who could easily be taken advantage of.

In Constantinople, young Victor went to work, selling shoestrings door to door. Either there was no market for shoestrings or he suddenly lacked confidence in himself, because he found it impossible to make a sale. He felt like a failure, unable to contribute to the financial well-being of his family. He finally came home to his father in tears, confessing his failure. Mark empathized with his son's suffering and found him another job, selling mineral water to neighborhood drugstores. This drew upon my father's successful experience in Tiflis finding mineral water for his mother. He most likely brought home some of the mineral water that he was selling to drugstores.

For whatever reason, this job suited him much better than the role of door-to-door shoestring salesman. Perhaps it was because he dealt with businessmen instead of housewives, or perhaps he simply had a product that people needed. In any event, my father's business career had begun in earnest now, and the setback with the shoestrings would be the only failure he encountered in the business world for the next eighty years.

Victor's formal education continued briefly in Constantinople. Mark found a tutor, a Frenchwoman who spoke no Russian but who agreed to tutor Victor and the rest of the children in German. The relationship, my father told me, was short-lived. The tutor got angry at him at some point, most likely due to his free-spirited ways—he was a lively child, despite all the hardships his family had been encountering—or perhaps it was due to his lack of interest in schooling of any kind. The tutor scolded him, thus becoming one of the few people on earth ever to give Victor Carter a verbal beating—only to watch him stalk out of the tutorial session in a huff, never to return. It was on this occasion that he made the statement to his father, since famous in family lore, "I don't take orders, I give them."

My grandfather, who prized education and culture in all forms, desperately wanted my father to continue his studies, but Victor steadfastly refused.

Through this time, life was "no picnic," Mark later recounted. One of Victor's sisters had fallen ill. A Turkish mob sought to kill Jews, and the Kartozhinskys had to hide in their house for three days until this pogrom subsided.

But Constantinople was simply a way station for my family en route to a new life. Ironically, Mark wrote, many Russian refugees viewed America as beneath their dignity. They thought the United States was a place for shopkeepers and tradespeople, but not for the crème de la crème of society, who belonged only in Paris or Berlin. Of course, those who opted to remain in Europe would fall victim to the Nazis in less than a generation. Mark and his family had no such pretensions about America. They knew that it was a land of freedom and opportunity. But where in America would they live? Who would help them?

While in Constantinople, my grandfather was corresponding with his brother-in-law Oscar Rudnick in the far-off land of California. Oscar was my father's uncle, the brother of my grandmother Fanya. Oscar's own story is worthy of a book: He came to the United States from Russia when he was just fourteen and traveled from his port of disembarkation, New York City, all the way to California, peddling small items along the way. By the time he arrived in what turned out to be his new home, Bakersfield, California, he owned horses and had amassed some wealth. His peddling became the foundation of a business in Bakersfield that would eventually become a multimillion-dollar packing plant.

So as Mark and Fanya weighed their options in Constantinople, Oscar was on his way to becoming an American millionaire, "making it" in the new land. Oscar wrote to my grandfather that if they would come to Los Angeles, Oscar, who was deeply devoted to Fanya, would take a year away from his business and help them get started. This was an extremely inviting offer, and one that my grandfather eventually accepted. The road to freedom had always pointed west—first to Tbilisi, and then to Constantinople. Now the next destination was in sight: the United States.

5

New York Days

My father was always passionate about life in the present. He was never a man of nostalgic feelings, someone who loved to talk about the "good old days" or how happy life had been in the past. Of course, he never left behind his memories of the violence he had witnessed as a boy in Rostov-on-Don. He also carried the emotional scars from the times in Tiflis and Constantinople when the family had struggled to survive. Memories like that, however, have nothing to do with nostalgia. These experiences are more like unhealed wounds, a lingering sense of underlying sadness that does not yield to the passage of time.

Over the course of his lifetime, my father said little to me about the journey from Constantinople to New York. We know from my grandfather's memoirs that it took twenty-eight days, that they sailed on the *King Alexander* with two thousand other immigrants, that my father turned twelve on that trip, and that they traveled second-class. The money that my grandfather had received from the bank in Constantinople, along with the hidden jewels, provided for a relatively comfortable journey across the sea. They did not have to travel in steerage, as did the overwhelming majority of immigrants to the United States during that period. My father told me that once they reached New York harbor and saw the Statue of Liberty on August 28, 1921, in his words, "We were home free."

In those days, the United States had strict quotas on the number of immigrants who were allowed to arrive in any one month. As a result, my father and his family got to enjoy that initial, welcoming view of the Statue of Liberty from New York harbor for three more days, until the first of September, when they were finally allowed to disembark. Because they had traveled in second class and not in steerage, they were spared the ordeal of going through Ellis Island and instead were allowed to board a smaller vessel that met the *King Alexander* in the harbor. As typically happened to immigrant families, American immigration officials shortened and simplified the family name. The Kartozhinskys suddenly became the Carters on their first day in their new land.

Mark recounted that his own brother Oscar, who had arrived in the United States four years earlier, came out on that smaller vessel to welcome the family to the New World.

My grandfather wrote:

> "The immigration officials released us, and at long last, we put our feet down on the solid soil of America. As we walked the streets in New York, the greatest city in the wonderful land of the United States, our happiness knew no bounds or chains. In every other land, we had seen human misery and destruction. Here hope and activity greeted us on every block. My brother took us to his home on Riverside Drive. We sat up until dawn crept into the city, a torrent of words pouring forth from all of our reflections on Russia, America, life, friends, the past, the future and us.[1]"

Now that the family was safely, if temporarily, ensconced in New York, Mark was confronted with the question that most immigrants face—how to make a living in a new land without speaking the language. Fortunately for Mark, he had the benefit of his brother Oscar's wealth and connections, and the family still had some money left from their passage to the United States. Therefore my grandfather had the wherewithal to buy

---

1. *Okay America*, pg. 22.

an existing business in New York, and he turned his attention to that possibility. He looked at various other hardware stores, but nothing seemed right. "Either the owner wanted too much money, or there were a hundred drawbacks to the business. I was growing increasingly edgy and unhappy," he wrote.

This is when the second Oscar in my family, the California Oscar, stepped in and changed the destiny of the Carter family. Fanya's brother Oscar Rudnick sent a telegram from his home in Bakersfield: "Come to Los Angeles; I will pay for your transportation." Mark wrote that he showed this telegram from the California Oscar to his brother, the New York Oscar, and sought his opinion. New York Oscar raged:

> "Why in the devil do you want to go to California? New York is life. California is wilderness. Here you have opportunity, culture. In California you will find a desert. In six months, you will come back." I insisted that thus far I had had a good time in New York, but I was spending money and not making any. Food was expensive and living costs were high. We needed to get settled in a home of our own, and place the children in school.

By then, several weeks into their New York experience, the joys of living in Manhattan were wearing thin. September 1921 was "miserably hot," in Mark's words, and he found people sleeping on rooftops and "drooping on doorsteps." He also disapproved of the "sea of pushcarts" he encountered. Since no appropriate business opportunities were presenting themselves in New York, my grandfather decided to accept California Oscar's invitation to come out West. The seven Carters traveled across the United States in two "drawing rooms," which Mark described as "high style."

"We said good-bye to my brother, who remained a New Yorker," Mark wrote, as he closed out the account of his New

York days, "and turned our thoughts and attention to the Far West. Many a pioneer whose ancestors had come to the United States from every country in Europe had made his way to California to seek his fortune. Now, the latest [addition] to the California melting pot was on its way."

On September 21, 1921, the Carter family arrived at Union Station in Los Angeles. Their new lives in America were now about to begin in earnest.

6

The Birth of Carter Hardware

CALIFORNIA AND MY FATHER were made for each other.

In 1921, Los Angeles was uncrowded, safe, and full of opportunity for a businessman like Mark who wanted to recreate his family fortune—and also for a young man like Victor who wanted to make his mark on the world. It had to be liberating to live in a society without the regulations and dangers of pre-Soviet Russia.

Mark wrote of the family's arrival: "There were no border guards, no secret police, no gendarmes. California was wonderful. I looked about at the clear blue sky, without any touch of the later-day smog, the flowers and trees, the easy-going people uncrazed by the New Yorkers' rush, and I breathed deeply. Los Angeles was for me."[1]

It was for my father, Victor, as well. When they arrived in 1921, he was twelve years old. He quickly learned English. He bicycled everywhere, finding his way around the growing city. He enrolled in junior high and then high school, but his attendance was spotty and his performance perfunctory—except for math, in which he was always exceptionally gifted. He was much more interested in learning about business.

The Carters settled into a rental house, but when the owner saw that the family included five children, he immediately ordered them to move. Mark wrote that he looked into housing in the Boyle Heights neighborhood east of downtown Los Angeles but found it a little "too Jewish" for his tastes. He did not want any part of a "ghetto," as he termed that then-vibrant Jewish

---

1. *Okay America*, page 28.

neighborhood. "America was not a place for ghettos," he wrote, "and I wanted American neighbors to help me learn the language as quickly as possible." He found and bought a house instead on Winfield Street, now called Eleventh Place, and that home quickly became the focal point of the neighborhood.

My father often told me how every Friday night his mother would encourage him and his sisters to invite all of their friends over for dinner and conversation. With five children and their friends, every Friday night was a source of enormous joy for Fanya. The entire family therefore had plenty of opportunity to hone their English-speaking skills. Although some of his sisters and his parents maintained Russian accents throughout their lives, my father learned to speak unaccented English.

Mark had safely conducted his family across Eastern Europe, the Atlantic, and the American continent, and he had bought a home, but he still had not determined how he was going to make a living. While he was still looking around Los Angeles for a suitable building to rent for his first store, Oscar Rudnick invited him to move to Bakersfield, where Oscar lived with his wife and eleven children, and where they operated a slaughterhouse. Oscar suggested that Mark invest a thousand dollars in cattle and become a rancher.

The experience was unsuccessful. As Mark's expertise was in the hardware business, it did not take him long to decide to make his way as the owner of a hardware store in Los Angeles. All of his new friends counseled against such a move, he wrote in his memoirs. They urged him to spend three years working as a clerk in someone else's store, learning how business was conducted in America, and learning the language. Mark would have none of it. He ignored the negative advice and rented a storefront that became the first home of Carter Hardware. He paid the princely sum of three hundred dollars a month in rent, prompting those same friends to tell him that he would go broke in no time. Since he spoke little English and had few contacts in the business world, most people who knew him thought he had little chance of success. But as promised, Oscar Rudnick took a year off from his business interests in Bakersfield to help the Carters become established in Los Angeles. Oscar's help would prove invaluable in the process of getting Carter Hardware off the ground.

The store was a block away from Main Street in downtown Los Angeles, where business was centered at that time. The seemingly undesirable location of the store only added to the loud comments of the well-meaning friends and business contacts who thought my grandfather was nothing more than an "absolute greenhorn." Mark paid no attention to their negative counsel. Instead, he and son Victor made the store a success from the beginning. Certainly there were sleepless nights, but it was a substantial money-maker even from the start.

Mark began to learn English while waiting on customers in the store. He would hand them a catalog of hardware implements and say, "Show me." The customer would find the object in the catalog, and thus Mark learned the basics of conversational and business English. It turned out that there were plenty of Russian-speaking immigrants who were very pleased to trade with a shopkeeper who spoke their language and who could share with them news from the motherland. Los Angeles, a magnet for immigrants then as now, also boasted a large German population. My grandfather was fluent in German, from his days as a student at the University of Leipzig, and was able to offer the Germans, too, a sense of home. My grandfather wrote that he regretted that he did not speak Spanish and Japanese, so as to take advantage of acquaintance with those burgeoning ethnic communities, too.

In addition to the word of mouth that spread through the Russian and German communities, Mark created other marketing opportunities for himself. In one notable event, he and Oscar printed up handbills announcing the existence of the store and the prices for various items. When Mark attempted to affix these handbills to the wall of a carpenter's union hall, he was rudely and firmly informed that without a union "bug," or symbol, the handbills were not permitted. To his surprise and sly amusement, however, the next day, a trail of carpenters and other tradesmen made their way to Carter Hardware. The union bosses had left my grandfather's handbills all over the floor, where the tradesmen, attracted by the low prices advertised on those handbills, had no problem overlooking the absence of a union "bug."

The language of business was universal. My grandfather's ability to make a living selling hardware in Los Angeles was unhampered by his limited English or by the fact that the business was located on a side street. People had no problem traveling an extra block to Carter Hardware. Parking was easier and prices were lower. The other hardware stores charged an eighteen percent markup over cost; Carter Hardware charged only ten percent. Low prices, a wide variety of goods, and friendly service—in your native language, if you happened to speak Russian or German—made the store an irresistible proposition for tradespeople and homeowners alike. Carter Hardware never had a losing year, often grossed in excess of a million dollars a year in sales, and never suffered from labor strife. When Mark sold the store, he gave each of his longtime employees a substantial gift.

One of the main reasons for the rapid success of Carter Hardware was my father's contributions. Victor was far more interested in the hardware business than in his schooling. He finally dropped out for good at age sixteen. In later years, he came to believe deeply in the importance of education. He became a voracious reader in many fields—today you would call him an information junkie. He received an honorary degree from Tel Aviv University, where he was president for several terms, and he became a major donor to many educational institutions, in the United States and in Israel. In his teenage years, though, my father had neither the time nor the inclination for education.

He simply moved too fast and had too much to do at the store. He was waiting on customers, ordering and negotiating with suppliers, delivering items—a blur of motion, contentedly running around the store with hundred-pound containers of nails, as he frequently told me. Life was a source of great happiness, at home, at the store, and in his personal life, as he took advantage of the freedom that America offered.

In the United States, then as now, freedom for a young man revolved around having a car of one's own. Somehow my father scraped the money together to buy a car. He raced that car at high speeds all over the streets of Los Angeles when he was just fifteen and sixteen years old. He smoked. He chased girls. He was having a sensational time, especially when compared with his experiences in Russia. His best friend in those years was his uncle George, who was my grandfather Mark's youngest sibling. Although George was technically Victor's uncle, they were just a year apart in age, and they were almost like brothers. George was a wild cut-up of a guy, and he and my dad got into a lot of mischief together.

When my father felt he had conquered Los Angeles, he looked for even greater adventures elsewhere. When he was about fifteen, he ran away from home and got a job aboard a ship in San Francisco. This was the era of Jack London and other adventure writers, and my father was heeding the call to the sea that so many young men followed in those days. "Adventure" for my father turned into a job peeling potatoes, not exactly what he had in mind. The company that ran the ship took pity on him and called his mother, who had been terrified when he disappeared. She said, "Come home, son." Thus ended this early romance with the high seas.

Back at Carter Hardware, my father's natural leadership abilities placed him in constant conflict with both his father and with the store manager, who eventually left because he was tired of competing with Victor to run the show. When not in school, my father spent practically every waking moment at the store, with two brief exceptions. These were his San Francisco shipboard adventure and an apprenticeship as a clerk at a local bank.

Mark considered himself an expert on how to run a hardware store, how to buy and sell, how to treat customers. And yet Victor, still in his teens, was already convinced that he knew better than his father. When, for instance, a competing hardware store moved into their neighborhood, Mark worried about all the business they would lose. Victor, by contrast, took the "invasion" of the neighborhood by a rival as an exciting business challenge.

"Let's lower our prices," Victor would say. "Let's give things away. Let's make it exciting to come to our store! Let's not worry about the competition! Let's be creative!" And with this joyous attitude, he would go about doing exactly that.

My father loved serving the customers. He deeply enjoyed being the quickest in the store to get them whatever they wanted. He prided himself on knowing the merchandise, so that he could recommend exactly what people needed. He could add up sums quickly in his head. Like his father, he had the ability to be both jovial and professional, to recognize the customers' needs and satisfy them promptly.

Victor and Mark both had the ability to make customers feel glad about returning to the store. People knew they were welcome guests at Carter Hardware. My father could remember countless details about the personal lives of the customers. Someone would come in and he'd say, "Oh, I'm so happy to see you! Where have you been? How's your wife, Sadie? How are the kids? Have you had that new baby yet?" In short, my father helped the business succeed by demonstrating genuine interest in and a sincere love for his customers—a vital aspect of his personality that would catapult him to the top.

In six short years, from his twelfth birthday until just before his eighteenth, my father had truly grown into manhood. He and his father had learned to make their way in a new land, speaking in a new language. They had started a new business, against all odds and against the advice of many well-meaning individuals. Although they had strong differences, they had learned to work together enough to make the store a huge success. My father had grown up fast, and now he was speeding into adulthood. His professional life was already secure, even though he was not out of his teens. How he handled his personal life with similar dispatch is at the heart of the next chapter.

7

Tijuana

MY FATHER'S TEENAGE YEARS took place against the backdrop of the Roaring Twenties, a time when a sense of exuberance was sweeping the entire nation. The "war to end all wars" was over, ushering in what many believed would be a perpetual era of peace and prosperity. The 1920s, therefore, were an exceptionally joyous time in American history, an era of accomplishment, daring, and fun. Charles Lindbergh crossed the Atlantic in 1927, when my father was eighteen. Flapper girls danced the Charleston and wore outfits that revealed more skin than ever before. Rivers of bootleg gin cascaded into nightclubs, speakeasies and private homes. The stock market was exploding—people were buying in the morning and making fortunes by the time they sold in the afternoon. In the 1920s, America was a party, and it looked as though the party would go on forever.

This is the America into which my father had arrived. As mentioned, school held little attraction for him. He attended Belmont High School and had received a work permit that would allow him to spend his afternoons and weekends at the store. In so doing, he was simply following a family tradition. Mark had gone to work for his grandfather at the age of twelve or thirteen, and hardware had been the family business for generations. So it was more comfortable, and more natural, for my father to log long hours at the store, where he felt at home, rather than at school, where his limited English—and limited patience for sitting still—were embarrassing hindrances.

Victor was a young man in a hurry—to help build Carter Hardware and to get his own life started. He was a favorite with the customers, who appreciated the fact that he could converse with them in Russian, or a few words of Japanese, or German, or Spanish, or even English, as the situation dictated. They loved the fact that he would run, not walk, to get them whatever they needed, hoist hundred-pound kegs of nails, and generally do whatever had to be done to satisfy them. Customers translated Victor's warm feelings for them into repeat sales and rapid growth for the business.

One of the regular customers at Carter Hardware was the man who would become my maternal grandfather, a builder named Morris Zucker. Homeowners and other do-it-yourselfers made up a respectable proportion of Carter Hardware's customer base. Like any hardware store, though, Carter Hardware relied on contractors, builders, tradesmen, and other professionals for the bulk of its business. Morris Zucker was fascinated with this young man who was so bright, who had the ability to add columns of figures in his head, who could quickly lay his hands on any article in the store, and who had a great gift for communicating with people. Morris developed the idea that he would bring Victor to his house and maybe marry off one of his daughters to this young man with such a promising future.

Morris invited Victor and Fanya to a meeting at his home one evening in 1927 to discuss the possibility of building a beautiful new home for the Carter family. After all, they had now been living in the United States for about six years. They were "making it" in the business world. So the time had come, Morris Zucker emphasized, for the Carters to build a beautiful new home.

The idea was practical. Mark and Fanya were raising four girls and a boy in a relatively small house, and by now they had the financial wherewithal for a considerably nicer home. So Fanya agreed to meet Morris, not only a builder but a Carter Hardware customer, to discuss such a venture.

Morris went home and told his family that Victor Carter and his mother were coming over to talk about a new house. Adrea, then seventeen, knew plenty about Victor Carter and Carter Hardware. My grandfather-to-be must have mentioned this remarkable young man to her on many occasions. She had just gotten out of high school and was not sure what she was going to do with her life. Morris did well enough as a builder, but at that time the family did not have the means to send her to college. Her brother was a pharmacist and her sister had graduated from the University of Southern California, but the family's savings well had run dry. Adrea took a job briefly as a secretary, but that did not work out—because the boss chased her around the office!

Adrea grasped that Victor Carter was a special young man, and she had been through enough dating experiences to know who she was and what she wanted in a husband. So she did what she could to make that "business" visit a memorable one for Victor. She had her sister sew her into a red velvet pillowslip that she had turned into a dress. The pillowslip had fringe on it, and it highlighted her great figure extremely well. When the Carters arrived, seventeen-year-old Adrea sashayed down the steps wearing that red velvet pillowslip and offered my father a cup of tea.

It was all over in a flash.

Fascinated by this beautiful girl in red velvet, Victor followed her into the kitchen, and they talked the rest of the evening. They went out on a date—just one date—and that date was a huge success, too. He said to her, "I have vacation time coming. Will you go to Tijuana with me? We can get married."

The issue of the house that my maternal grandfather was to build for Mark and Fanya quickly was overshadowed by what

Victor and Adrea did next. At eighteen and seventeen, they could never have been married legally in California without parental permission.

Mexico was another story.

Back then, couples did not need parental permission to go to Tijuana and get married. Five days after their initial meeting, the two of them eloped to Mexico.

Victor had told her to pack a bag and be ready Friday evening. Adrea told her sister, Charlotte, "Please don't embarrass me! If he doesn't show up to pick me up, don't ever mention it again."

When the end of the workweek arrived, my father pulled up in his car in front of Adrea's house. He drove a pretty sporty-looking coupe at the time, which fit both his personality and hers. She was wearing a gray silk dress, and ever after my father loved it when she wore gray. They drove from Los Angeles to Mexico without telling a soul aside from Charlotte where they were going or what they were going to do.

Leaving Los Angeles at six o'clock, given the state of the roads between Los Angeles and the Mexican border, they could not have arrived much before midnight. They roused the Mexican equivalent of a justice of the peace from his sleep, explained that they had eloped, and were married.

And that marriage lasted seventy-five years.

It was destiny that the two of them met and married in this manner. My father knew from the first moment he saw Adrea that this was the woman with whom he wanted to spend the rest of his life. She was ready to get married, as well, and after the buildup that her father had given her about Victor, she was ready to go, sewn into that red fringed pillowslip. It was a case of mutual attraction, and it turned into a love story for all time.

Newlyweds Adrea and Victor Carter, 1929.

Mark and Fanya were worried sick about Victor when he did not return home that Friday night. Just two years earlier he had run away from home and ended up peeling potatoes. Who knew what kind of adventure—or danger—he had gotten himself into this time?

The families found out when Victor and Adrea sent a telegram to Mark. Charlotte hadn't said a word.

My parents spent a honeymoon week in Tijuana before they came home. They took time to see the sights, to attend the bullfights, go to the horse races—whatever was the most exciting thing in town, my father wanted to do it, and my mother wanted to go along. They found the best restaurants and they visited the hottest spots—it was a heady time for a young, newly married couple out on their own, incredibly romantic and totally in keeping with the natures of both Victor and Adrea.

I see their impulsive decision to get married as a reflection of the times. My mother was a flapper. She wore short skirts, she loved to dance and won a dance competition, she came in second in a singing competition and was a gifted pianist as well. She loved having a great time. And here came this young man who was certainly a fun-loving guy, a high-spirited individual, one who had already earned the respect of her father, which back in those days still meant something for young women. They were an ideal match—perfect for the times and each other.

My father's romantic nature was tempered by his business responsibilities. After their honeymoon in Tijuana, they crossed the border and headed back to Los Angeles to celebrate the news with their extremely surprised families. But first Victor had a surprise for Adrea, one that she probably didn't care for all that much. Along the way, between San Diego and Los Angeles, he had arranged business meetings and visits with Carter Hardware clients. Victor was not going to let the little matter of a honeymoon interfere with his continuing responsibilities to grow Carter Hardware.

I imagine my mother, sitting in the car, waiting for her new husband to conclude his business and get back on the road. I believe my father was destined to be a loving and caring husband. Yet he was certainly not one to let romance get in the way of his business responsibilities.

The funny thing about their honeymoon is that, while they most certainly consummated the marriage—again, the two of them were very high-energy, fun-loving people—they were still simply getting acquainted. It's not like today, when you may know your partner for a year or more and may even live with the person for some time before you commit. Back then, my parents' honeymoon was a journey of discovery about the other person's nature, an opportunity for the two of them to discover exactly to whom they had committed to spend the rest of their lives. And of course the trip represented my father's pragmatic nature. He could take the vacation time coming to him, get married, see his clients, all in about a week, and then be back at the store, without missing a beat.

I have to give my mother enormous credit for going along with the whole thing. I admire the courage of a woman who was willing to say, after just one date, "Okay, what the heck." She knew that her options were limited and that college was not possible. So here came the star of Carter Hardware, a young man who already earned a living and who could give her a reasonably bright future. He sounded like a good catch. That's the kind of people my parents were—"high risk" people, willing to take chances in life. They were ready to do interesting and different things, and in that manner they lived their entire lives.

I once had a conversation about this period in my father's life with Adele Faulkner, a successful businesswoman and one of the leading decorators in Los Angeles. She had attended Belmont High with Victor, and she told me, "You know, your father was quite a guy." I asked her what she meant by that. She said she meant that my father had that indefinable *something*, that magic, that pushes a person ahead of the pack. Even as a teenager, Victor showed that he was willing to take a chance. He clearly had imagination and he believed in himself.

My father had a lot of girlfriends when he was in high school. He was an aggressive young man, he wanted to see what life was all about, and he certainly always loved women. He managed to get a certain amount of experience with women before he met my mother. Adrea was very cute, very attractive. Her older brother, the pharmacist, would set her up with different friends of his. She was always ready for a party, very peppy, and with a lot of spirit. So when she and my father met, even though they were both very young, they had plenty of experience in terms of meeting other people and dating, and they had a pretty strong sense of what they wanted and what they didn't want in their lives.

As the Roaring Twenties roared on, my parents seemed to have it all—a happy marriage, a successful work life, and with the birth of my brother, Bobby, the beginning of a family life. The calendar was about to turn for the Carters and for the nation, however. The stock market crash of 1929 ushered in the era of the Great Depression, and it also marked the official beginning of adulthood for my father. Time was drawing its curtain on the age of innocence, both for the nation and for my parents. My father's years of responsibility at home and at work were about to begin.

8

Conflicts at Work

SHORTLY AFTER VICTOR AND ADREA WERE MARRIED, on July 15, 1928, things began to change in important ways for them. First, my grandmother Fanya passed away within a year of their marriage. She went to the hospital for a routine procedure that resulted in a blood clot, perhaps due to a mistake by the doctor. At that time there was no method for dealing with a blood clot of that type, and Fanya died within a matter of days. Today, that kind of medical situation would probably not have been life-threatening, but the knowledge, techniques and medications available today did not exist at the time.

My grandmother's death was devastating for my father, of course, because the two of them had been so close—in Russia, on the road, and in their new life in the United States. Gone were all those carefree, fun-loving evenings when my grand-mother would say to Victor, "Bring all your friends over! Let's have a party!"

If the 1920s had been the age of frivolity, then the 1930s, which began for my father with the loss of his mother, were a different era altogether. This would be a time of painful conflicts and challenges. My parents' marriage was always strong, yet a series of events at work and at home would bring enormous emotional suffering to my father for many years. The death of my grandmother may have pushed Victor and Adrea closer to one another and helped to cement the bond between them that would last for three-quarters of a century.

Mark remarried after Fanya's death. His new wife, Reva, was the widow of a leading member of the Jewish community in Los Angeles. They met through friends and developed a close rela-tionship.

Relations between Victor, on the one side, and Mark and Reva, on the other, grew complicated when Reva brought some members of her family into the business and also increased the role she played in its management. My father saw this development as a challenge to be solved creatively rather than as some kind of insurmountable problem. He found ways to work harmoniously with Reva's sons and other relatives.

In the early 1930s, Los Angeles had begun its inexorable spread to the west. My father conceived the idea of opening a branch of Carter Hardware on Western Avenue, just west of downtown. Mark refused because he did not think that customers wanted to shop anywhere but downtown. Victor was stymied by his father's refusal, and the branch on Western never materialized. Ironically, Victor's uncle George liked my father's idea of going west. George opened a hardware store on La Brea, even farther west than Western, and did quite well there.

My father and grandfather disagreed frequently over the question of advertising and promotion. From his earliest days in the business, Victor recognized the importance of spending money on advertising. Mark was no stranger to the value of advertising and promotion, but he was occasionally averse to risk and thought my father wanted to spend too much money on advertising. Similarly, Victor would always want to order in greater bulk than Mark would feel comfortable doing.

The management conflicts came to a head in 1935, when Victor had the store redesigned. He created a perch, a kind of gallery window, from which he could sit and watch every aspect of the operation—the showroom floor, the financial operations on the second floor, the warehouse, all of it. Not only could he see everyone and everything, but everyone could also see him. There would be no question about who was running the business when you looked up to that high perch and saw Victor looking down on the empire he had built with his father.

Reva thought it would be more appropriate if she took that "catbird seat." This was the event that convinced my father to leave the business and go off on his own, a development that had been a long time coming. Victor most likely assumed that Mark would retire at some point and finally turn the reins over to him. Without the conflict with Reva I don't think my father would ever have left Carter Hardware and gone on to accomplish even greater things in business. So these developments amounted to a blessing in disguise.

To leave a family business under these circumstances, however, without any clear sense of where to go or what to do next, was not easy. But unlike many businesspeople, my father was never afraid to take a long period of time to lie fallow, recharge his batteries, consider his options, and then strike out in a new direction altogether. And that is exactly what he did next.

His days at Carter Hardware were over, and it was time to start a new business. In the meantime, there were challenges at home as well—serious challenges.

9

My Brother, Bobby

IN LATER YEARS, MY PARENTS would always refer to themselves as "the lucky Carters." People of their generation were not given to the kind of introspection and self-analysis in which later generations would immerse themselves. Instead, they were content to see themselves as fortunate people—and for the most part they were fortunate indeed.

In one particular area of their lives, though, they were considerably less fortunate, and all of my father's intensity, focus, connections, and general stick-to-it-iveness were unable to bring about a happy result. I refer to the saddest experience in the life of my family, the illness and eventual passing of my brother, Bobby.

Bobby was born in 1929, less than a year after my parents' sudden elopement to Tijuana. He was my older brother, and I always thought of him as an angel, the epitome of loving-kindness, a treasure to all of us and to anyone who knew him. He seemed perfectly healthy at birth. It wasn't until he was two or three years old that anything unusual could be noted about him. He began to fall, so often that my mother eventually took him to the family doctor to determine what was wrong. It turned out that my brother had muscular dystrophy.

There was and is no cure for muscular dystrophy. This did not keep my parents from trying everything they could think of to help Bobby. They brought him to doctor after doctor, tinkered with his diet, tried chiropractic when most people in America either knew nothing of chiropractic or thought that it was quackery. They gave everything they could to Bobby, but nothing made a difference in terms of his long-term survival.

The change in my parents' lives from the flapper era of the 1920s to the Depression era of the 1930s could not possibly have been more profound. Just a few years earlier, they had been carefree teenagers with few responsibilities. And then, as the decade turned, everything in their lives was transformed. My father was now working full-time at the store, with the attendant stresses and strains of working in a family business. Some building was still going on in the Depression years, but it took a great deal of creativity on the part of Victor and Mark to keep Carter Hardware thriving in those difficult days. And certainly my mother's life was transformed as well—she went from being a flapper girl who danced the Charleston to a stay-at-home mom with a terminally ill son.

In those days my father was rarely home. He had to spend evenings and weekends at the store. Much of his considerable energy was consumed by the question of how to keep the business successful as the Depression deepened. So it fell to my mother to take care of Bobby, a beautiful young child suffering from a horrible degenerative disease. Bobby's illness cast a shadow over what should have been the happy carefree first years of my parents' marriage. They had no particular training for coping with an illness of this magnitude—back then, nobody did. They did the best they could for Bobby, bringing over those friends they considered capable of handling the sight of a young boy who was so sick. Not everybody was up to this, of course, and my parents thought carefully about whom they brought home to see Bobby. Fortunately, they had the financial ability to provide him with a full-time nurse and companion, so he was never alone.

Bobby was quick-minded, like my father, had a great sense of humor, and possessed a creative and discerning mind. He had the full range of hobbies and interests that most boys had—he

Victor and his son, Bobby.

loved baseball, and especially the Brooklyn Dodgers, and he was almost delirious with joy when one of my father's friends brought him a baseball autographed by the entire Dodgers team. He loved listening to the radio and would listen for hour after hour with his nurse to news broadcasts and the great radio serials of the day—dramas like Lux Radio Theater, the "scary" shows, the comedy shows with Jack Benny or Edgar Bergen. He and I especially liked "Let's Pretend" fairy tales on Saturday morning—that was our favorite show to enjoy together. I came along four years after Bobby was born. My mother had experienced a miscarriage between Bobby's birth and her pregnancy with me, and my parents went to great lengths to prepare properly for this third pregnancy, which they knew would be their last chance to have another child. My mother was given lime juice and all sorts of concoctions and observed special dietary restrictions so that she would be able to get pregnant and then carry a healthy child to term.

I loved Bobby from the earliest time I was able to understand that he was my older brother. I think of him as an absolute saint brought down from heaven to Earth to teach us all about love. He was extraordinarily good-natured, and I don't remember ever hearing him complain about his illness, even in his later years, as the muscular dystrophy robbed him of his ability to perform even the simplest of physical functions. I spent hours with Bobby in his room in the back of our house, playing cards, listening to the radio, or just talking with him.

Back then, my mother's parents lived next door to us, and my aunt and uncle lived next door to them, so we had a family enclave. That sense of family was important in a situation like ours, and the relatives would all come over and visit Bobby. My mother had an occasional friend who was courageous enough to sit right down with him and not be frightened by his illness. I had some friends like that, too. I'm still close with Lorraine Baron, one of my friends from that time, more than sixty-two years ago. She was willing to come into Bobby's room and visit with him. This was not for the faint of heart, yet he was so funny, smart and upbeat that many felt inspired by his company. As time passed, Bobby's falling gave way to an inability to walk, and then he would lie in bed, his ability to move diminishing as time passed and his condition worsened. At the end, he could barely move his eyes.

Bobby's longtime caretaker was Mrs. Dawson, who had had polio as a child and walked with a limp. Mrs. Dawson couldn't have been more different politically or culturally from our family—she was a Texas Republican who listened to the Grand Ole Opry every Saturday night, living amidst a family that loved classical music and idolized Franklin Roosevelt. She and Bobby had many heated political discussions, but they always shared mutual respect. We were devoted listeners to FDR's Fireside Chats. Mrs. Dawson, teeth clenched, would leave the room when the president came on the air. For all their political differences, the relationship between Bobby and Mrs. Dawson was one of poignant devotion, and she seldom left his side during the twelve years she was with us.

Bobby passed away when he was seventeen. I was thirteen. After that, my parents seldom talked about him. It was just too painful to bring up his memory, and it didn't really fit with their nature, that Zen-like mentality in which they were most interested in the current moment. The loss was so painful that they could not find words with which to discuss it. They did not dwell on the topic of Bobby's life, but I know it upset them to the core of their beings.

My parents never discussed Bobby's illness with me when I was a child. It was as if they needed to put aside thoughts of

Victor and Adrea, daughter Fanya and husband Jack.

Bobby in order to do what they were doing—be married, work on the business, raise me. And it was too bad, in a way, because as a child I was left to struggle through it myself. I did not really know how to handle it very well. I think that my own spirituality has been formed by that experience, because Bobby was really like some kind of translucent soul, a disembodied spirit.

He wasn't really in that non-functioning body of his. And yet he was such a strong spirit and had such a big heart and soul that you had to relate to him, not as a physical being, but on some other level. His mind was so bright and his heart was so big and his soul was so present that you had to transcend to really experience him. My experience as Bobby's younger sister formed me in some way that came to the fore later on as I developed my own journey of consciousness and awareness.

There was never any talk about loss or mourning until my husband, Jack, came into the family many years later. When Jack arrived, he brought with him the skills and the sensitivity to bring up Bobby's name with me, and then with my parents, in an extraordinarily careful and loving way. Jack, an experienced and deeply caring psychoanalyst, recognized the level of hidden pain in my parents' lives because they lacked the vocabulary with which to discuss their loss. It was interesting to watch that process unfold, a process Jack had initiated out of his great love for my parents and for me. Jack talked to me a lot about Bobby and he helped me come to terms with the loss of a brother I loved dearly.

My parents began to mention Bobby's name once in a while, and they were able, after all those years, to begin to access, and perhaps to process, some of the pain they felt about his death and about their own impotence to change the course of Bobby's life. Until Jack came along, they had shut a door on the whole thing. My mother once said to me, "After that happened, nothing could hurt me anymore. I just decided I was going to enjoy my life, because the worst had happened to me that could happen to a person."

It was terrible for me, too, because my whole childhood was colored by the pain of trying to heal my brother and not being able to. I used to pray to the stars and pray to God and to the powers that be. And I was sure that my prayers and my thoughts that I shared with the stars were going to be answered somehow. It was painful and frustrating for all of us when our prayers were not answered.

My parents were not able to save Bobby's life, but instead of sinking into depression or blame, they turned their experience with Bobby into a passion to make the world a better place. It sounds like a cliché until you see everything that my father accomplished, both in the years of Bobby's lifetime and afterward. Bobby truly was an angel, and he inspired my parents, and me, and all who knew him. I still miss him terribly.

10

The Vimcar Years

MY FATHER TOOK "SABBATICALS" from business on three separate occasions—once, after leaving Carter Hardware; the second time after ceasing major operations at Vimcar; and the third time after selling Builders Emporium. I put the word "sabbaticals" in quotes because he did not cease all of his business activities during those periods of repose. Instead, for those blocks of time, he simply was not engaged in the day-to-day management of a specific company. Yet he was always following the business world carefully, watching trends, and considering his next steps.

After each of his career shifts, he did something extraordinary by the standards of most businesspeople—he took time off. Not a few weeks or a month or two, but more than a year each time. He used these protracted breaks to rejuvenate himself and think about what he wanted to do next. In 1937, he had returned from a fateful trip to Japan having made up his mind to leave the family business. So he left Carter Hardware and had the financial wherewithal to sit tight and think about what he really wanted to do next with his life. He was not yet thirty years old, and although the Depression raged on, he and Adrea were by now wealthy enough to take a sabbatical year, to continue to live nicely, and to provide medical care for Bobby, then seven years old.

My father considered all sorts of different business opportunities before he settled on the manufacture and distribution of steel sash, a new product just then coming into its own. Steel sash was a form of window frame that allowed occupants of homes and offices to open windows with a crank instead of the traditional method of lifting a heavy window. There was little

Victor in his office at Vimcar.

commercial construction during the Depression, but people still needed places to live, so residential construction continued. My father also sensed that at some point the economy would rebound and the pace of commercial building would rapidly increase. He felt that there was a great future in steel sash, because it was considerably cheaper to manufacture and install than traditional, handmade, wooden window frames. So he started a business around this particular product, and that business was called Vimcar, short for Victor M. Carter.

Vimcar came to life in a typical, nondescript-looking warehouse at 4041 Whiteside Street in East Los Angeles. The one thing that set the location apart was that Victor had the gardeners trim bushes into the shapes of the letters that spelled out VIMCAR. As a little girl visiting the company with my father, I always found it delightful to see those letters carved into the bushes. I had never seen anything like that before, and it was a source of great pride to me that they stood for my father's name and business.

Vimcar gave Victor his first opportunity to create his own enterprise, and he certainly made the most of it. The company's customers during this first phase of its existence were contractors building homes and commercial properties around the country. The business was a success from the start, and it grew rapidly as the economy in the late 1930s began to rebound. However, Vimcar would ultimately succeed not so much because my father had chosen a timely product (steel sash would be replaced in the postwar years by aluminum) but because of the facilities in which the steel sash was produced.

World War II started within a few years of the company's inception. Victor suddenly found himself with the single-most desirable commodity in the entire business world at that time: production capacity. Virtually everything that happened in industry during the early 1940s had to do with the war effort. When the United States entered the war, Vimcar entered its second phase, moving from a company that manufactured steel sash for building contractors to a company that manufactured whatever the government needed.

During the war, machine tools were extremely hard to come by, and little funding existed for the expansion of existing factories or the creation of new ones. So if you had industrial capacity—if you had the space, the equipment, and the people necessary to make things—you were in a very fortunate position. My father, by having left the sale of hardware for the business of manufacturing, had made essentially the most brilliant transition that any businessman could have hoped to make in those last days of the Depression. The Carter luck had struck again.

I remember my father flying frequently to Washington during the war to win new contracts for Vimcar. He would actually sleep on the steps of the government buildings where he was to meet with officials, so that he would be first in line when the doors opened in the morning, to have their ear and negotiate a deal. Vimcar's business expanded exponentially during World War II, not because Victor M. Carter had chosen the right product, but because he had taken his business career in the right direction.

A witness to my father's brilliance, foresight, toughness, and "people skills" is my first cousin Jeremy Berg, known as Jerry, who has always been like a brother to me. Jerry ran a successful scrap metal business in Southern California throughout his career, and he got his start working each summer for my father at Vimcar. Jerry's father, an attorney, had been in the scrap metal business along with his brothers, but he did not enjoy the business world. He was happiest when he had the leisure time to sit

At Vimcar Steel. Several names were handwritten on the original photo: "Jack (with cigar), Jim, Barney, Victor and his secretary Henrietta."

and read a good book, peruse a magazine, and ponder the great issues of the day. Jerry, even as a teenager, had a much more businesslike frame of mind, and Jerry's father would frequently say to him, "You're a Carter! You think just like them!"

Jerry first came to work for Vimcar around the time of his fourteenth birthday. Every summer, my father would put him to work in a different aspect of the plant. Jerry realizes now that his uncle Victor was deliberately giving him a business education by exposing him to as many aspects of business as possible. When Jerry was old enough, he would drive Victor to and from work, either from our home in Los Angeles or from summer homes in Santa Monica and the Malibu Colony. Along the way, Jerry got to see Victor in action.

My father had one of the first car phones installed in his black Cadillac convertible, back in the early 1940s. I can still remember his mobile number: JL 4-2674, and I can hear the voice of the mobile operator chiming through the telephone. "This is the mobile operator!" she would announce, and I knew it was my Dad. "JL 4-2674 is calling!" she'd say. This was necessary at the time in order to connect a mobile caller with a land line. My father's voice would then come booming over the wire. Typically, the purpose of his call was to let us know that he would be late for dinner.

Back then, as today, reception for a mobile phone was an issue. Jerry recalls that there was no service in the Santa Monica area for car phones, because car phones were so rare. Jerry and my father would race to work in the convertible. Once they had cleared a particular tunnel on Pico Boulevard, telephone service was available. Victor would be on the phone from that moment until they reached their destination. Between calls, he would take time to explain to Jerry what he was doing, what the other fellow was up to, and how he was handling the situations. Jerry attributes his success in business to the apprenticeship and education in negotiation and management that my father provided him.

My father's addiction to the phone was certainly an issue in my parents' marriage. When he got home from work, he would set the telephone on the dining room table, in case a business call came in. This annoyed my mother no end, and she would sometimes comment about the permanent dent he was creating in his forehead while he was talking on the phone.

When Jerry was apprenticing with my father, during the mid-to-late 1940s, my brother, Bobby, was nearing the end of his short life. Given his physical condition, a career in business was never open to him. So it's fair to say that Jerry fulfilled the role of surrogate son to my father, one whom Victor could teach the ways of business, as had been a Carter family tradition going back generations.

One might wonder why my father chose to bestow his business knowledge on his nephew instead of his daughter. In those days, girls were expected to marry well and have children instead of going into the business world. So my father shared his wisdom with Jerry instead of with me.

By the time Jerry came to work for my father during the summers, the war had ended and Vimcar had entered its third—and most lucrative—phase. After the war, the company's manufacturing operations ceased. My father recognized that there was more money to be made in postwar America as a jobber, or middleman, for essential hardware products. So he lined up suppliers of all kinds of necessary items for home and business construction and became the exclusive distributor for those companies. He now offered garage door hardware, door locks, and chrome items for bathrooms such as soap dishes and towel racks. His customers were large hardware stores and lumberyards, to whom he would sell these items wholesale, and large contractors, who needed the hardware for the homes and commercial buildings they were putting up.

After World War II, there was intense demand for new homes, office buildings, and factories. With his knack for choosing just the right mix of products (combined with the fabled Carter luck), Victor had exclusive agreements with manufacturers to sell *exactly what was needed* at a time when there was a frenzy of building in the country. He turned Vimcar into a nationwide sales and distribution firm for the hardware industry. (Actually, the "Carter luck" that friends and family exclaimed over was more often intuition combined with timing, savvy, and hard work. My father always did what it took to "get the job done," as he liked to say.)

Jerry recalls that everything about my father's approach to the business was innovative. This was as true of his shipping methods as it was in his approach to credit. For example, Vimcar sold many door locks to contractors building apartment buildings in New York City. The cost of freight would have taken virtually all of the profit out of the deal. So Victor hit upon the idea of shipping the door locks by boat to New York City, instead of doing the conventional thing and sending them by train or truck.

At the same time, Jerry recalls, my father had a highly personal approach to issuing credit. Typically, Vimcar would advertise around the country in the classified ad sections of newspapers, seeking independent salesmen to offer the Vimcar line to customers. An order would come in from one of the out-of-town sales reps. The credit department, where Victor had positioned Jerry one summer, would look up the buyer in Dun and Bradstreet, a service that reported the credit worthiness of every business in the nation. If the customer's credit was poor, the credit office rejected the order. At most businesses, that's where things would have stopped. At Vimcar, things were different. My father insisted that all rejected credit applications be funneled to his desk, an extraordinary request by a CEO. He would review those rejected orders, and on occasion, he would overrule the credit office and approve the order. One time, Jerry asked why.

"We build in one-half of one percent of all sales for bad debts," my father explained to Jerry. "If it's the middle of the month and we are running less than that, I'll take a chance on the order."

Business wisdom like this built Vimcar into a powerhouse and, again, had a profound effect on Jerry's later business success.

Victor's hiring practices in general were unusual for the day. He hired many Hispanic workers, something that other employees were often loath to do. He also hired many Japanese workers immediately after World War II, which was truly extraordinary. Most people in this country viewed the Japanese— *all* Japanese, even those who lived here in the United States throughout all of World War II—as the enemy, and had no interest in having anything to do with them, personally or professionally. My father's connection to the Japanese-American community had begun in the early 1920s, when he began to serve Japanese customers at Carter Hardware. His 1937 trip to Japan was one of the most fascinating and exciting of his life, and he always felt a deep affinity for the Japanese people. So when the war ended and Japanese workers were available, he hired them, without concern about their ethnicity. My father simply wanted to hire the best; he did not care about issues of race or what other people might think. This was typical—he had a boldness of spirit undeterred by fear of the opinions of others.

As the late 1940s came to a close, Victor recognized that the days for a middleman like Vimcar were numbered. Companies that made the sort of hardware Vimcar sold had begun to sell directly to hardware stores, lumberyards, and contractors, Vimcar's bread-and-butter clients. So there was not much of a future as a jobber in an economy in the process of wiping out the middleman. My father closed Vimcar on highly successful financial terms, though. Some of the companies with whom he had exclusive distribution contracts had to buy back those contracts at a very high price. Victor bought several of the companies whose products he sold, and he essentially bestowed two of those companies on two of his most valuable people at Vimcar, making them extremely wealthy in the process.

My father emerged from the Vimcar years with three important results. First, he was able to establish the kinds of banking relationships and credit he would need for his later ventures. Second, he was able to close out the business profitably. And finally, he had established himself as a highly successful and competent businessman in his own right. With Vimcar, he stepped out of the shadow of the family business. The Vimcar era ended as it had begun, with my father taking the second of his major sabbatical periods. During this time he was again rejuvenated, after the many years of hard work at Vimcar, and began to think about what to do next.

It was the early 1950s. Once again GIs were returning from war—this time in Korea—and getting married, starting families, and buying homes in newly developed suburbs such as the San Fernando Valley to the north of Los Angeles. Meeting the needs of these new families would be the next step in Victor Carter's career.

11

Builders Emporium

IN THE LATE 1940S, my father noticed the confluence of two important trends in the hardware industry. The first was the oncoming demise of the middleman, as the companies that had done business with Vimcar were now beginning to sell directly to hardware stores, contractors, and homeowners. The second trend involved the return of veterans from World War II, and later the Korean War. The most important thing for the servicemen returning from conflict was to establish a sense of normalcy. The government made it as easy as possible for veterans to start their new lives by enabling them to buy inexpensive homes with no money down.

Homes in the San Fernando Valley, north of Los Angeles, that today sell for three-quarters of a million dollars or more became available to their first owners, returning GIs, for little more than their signature on loan documents. Across the country, millions of GIs were getting married, starting families, and buying houses. My father wisely recognized that the future of the hardware business would be to sell directly to these new homeowners.

As he was winding down Vimcar, one particular creditor, a small, ailing hardware store in the San Fernando Valley, was unable to pay its bills. My father, conscious of the twin trends outlined above, recognized a unique opportunity. He decided to accept ownership of that hardware store as a settlement of the debt. The store wasn't much, but with my father's vision, it was about to become something legendary.

The store was called Builders Emporium, and when Victor Carter took it over, it was a small storefront operation selling hardware to the burgeoning new class of homeowners. Its clientele were do-it-yourselfers—men who wanted to increase their sense of domestic tranquility by improving the fairly simple houses they had been able to acquire. They wanted to add decks, extra rooms, workshops, and barbecue pits to their new homes, and they needed hardware and materials to make their domestic dreams come true.

My father combined his retail experience from Carter Hardware with his wholesale experience from Vimcar and turned Builders Emporium into the most extraordinary hardware store the nation had ever seen. Today, we take "big box" home improvement stores like The Home Depot or Lowe's for granted. During the 1940s, however, there was no such thing as a self-service hardware store. Typically, when you went into a hardware store back then, you had the same shopping experience that you might have had at Carter Hardware in the 1920s. The clerk would greet you and you would tell him what you wanted. He would get it for you and ring up the sale. Builders Emporium under my father was stunningly different in a number of important ways. First, it was huge. The store covered a vast amount of space at the increasingly busy intersection of Sepulveda and Oxnard Boulevards in the Valley, a convenient location for tens of thousands of these new homeowners, as well as contractors and builders putting up even more homes. Because the store was so large, it offered not just the nuts and bolts and hammers and nails that you would find in a typical hardware store. It offered outdoor furniture equipment, kitchen items, fishing tackle. You could find much more than nuts and bolts at Builders Emporium.

Victor designed Builders Emporium not like a hardware store but like a supermarket, itself a relatively new idea in American marketing and one that my father greatly admired. The supermarket approach encouraged shoppers to wander the aisles at leisure and come away with not just the few items that they had originally thought to buy but with "impulse purchases" as well. A hardware store designed to allow customers to roam freely was a brilliant innovation, and it was my father's idea.

Since customers had the freedom to purchase items not on their shopping lists, they would buy much more at Builders Emporium than at the traditional hardware stores. In addition, the store sold everything for considerably less than you could find it anywhere else. This was a business practice that my father had carried over from Carter Hardware, which sold all of its items at a substantial discount compared with its competitors. In addition, Builders Emporium offered, by the standards of the time, large parking facilities. You could park your car on any side of the building and have easy access to the store. Since most hardware stores in the United States were run along the same lines as the tiny storefront that my father had taken over, the amount of parking made Builders Emporium an even more desirable location for do-it-yourselfers and professional contractors alike.

Lower prices, the freedom to choose whatever you wanted without having to be waited on by a salesclerk, ample parking, salespeople in every department to offer guidance—these were among the many innovations at Builders Emporium. My father took things a step further. Unlike his situation at Carter Hardware, he had complete freedom to do anything he wanted in terms of marketing. So he made Builders Emporium the first of what today's marketers call "destination stores." In other words, my father made it fun for the whole family to come to shop. There were free balloons, lemonade, hot dogs, and entertainment for the kids. There was a 99-cent table that offered amazing bargains.

Turning Builders Emporium into a large, airy "destination" store meant that while the kids were outside munching on their hot dogs, dad was buying a lot more tools, equipment, and supplies than he might have planned to purchase. Mom was checking out the kitchenware and small appliances—tableware, glasses, everything for the home. If you were purchasing a large item, an employee would bring it right to your car.

The philosophy that drove my father's marketing efforts was part business and part spiritual—he understood that the more you give away, the more that comes back to you. It was a key principle in his life. When he gave out free lemonade and hot dogs, he was making the people feel comfortable and at home. And they responded to his generosity by buying in remarkable quantities.

While I was taking undergraduate courses at the University of California, Los Angeles, a classmate and I spent one summer working for my father at Builders Emporium. I worked in the department that sold kitchen items and small appliances, and I would answer questions from the customers about the various products we offered. I felt a serious responsibility to pull my own weight and never to take advantage of the fact that I was the boss's daughter. I enjoyed the experience of working in my father's store, yet I realized I wasn't interested in entering the business world at that time. Working there definitely brought me closer to my father. I did not see much of him, because he was usually in the office and busy with other things. Yet I did gain a better understanding of what his life at work was like.

As a result of the success of Builders Emporium, the land in the area around Sepulveda and Oxnard grew in value. Victor wisely invested in that land, buying a drive-in movie theater that he developed into a highly profitable real estate venture. He continued to expand Builders Emporium and also managed the last pieces of Vimcar from his office in the store.

My father was hardly an individual to remain confined in his office, however. His ebullient nature, combined with his hands-on approach to leadership, caused him to leave his office constantly, to wander the aisles and see what was going on—what was selling, how the various salesclerks were doing, what needed to go and what needed to be reordered. Again, he was decades ahead of the "experts." Today, business schools preach the virtues of "MBWA"—Management By Walking Around. Victor was practicing MBWA well before many of today's business professors were born! He knew that there was no substitute for seeing with his own eyes exactly what was going on in every aspect of the business.

My father's emphasis on keeping his eye on all aspects of the business was influenced by the fact that the first person he chose to manage Builders Emporium grossly overbought inventory for the store. So he spent the first months of the store's existence clearing out that entire surplus inventory, and eventually clearing out that manager as well. He also took a deep personal interest in the employees, and it was his habit to give out Christmas bonuses personally to all of them. He would sit in the back of the store and greet each individual, thus demonstrating to them (as if they did not already know it) his care, compassion, and appreciation for them, which they returned in full measure.

It had to be exhilarating for my father to be his own boss at Builders Emporium, to re-create on a vastly larger scale the business success of Carter Hardware. Victor would never have wanted to go head to head against his father's store. The distance between the two stores was such that there would have been no overlap among their customer bases. If you lived in the Valley, you would not drive downtown for your hardware, and vice versa. So Victor always maintained a respectful distance from Mark and the family business.

My father had a very strong sense of right and wrong, which evidenced itself in both his philanthropic work and his business morals. "You have to be straight, you have to be lawful, you have to treat every transaction in a fair way," he told a *Los Angeles Times* reporter in 1987. "Integrity is very important." Certainly, no one ever questioned his integrity. His philosophy of business was not about making the last dollar; it was about making a deal that allowed both parties to walk away pleased, because he knew that he would be doing business with these same individuals again and again.

That philosophy was probably honed during his days at Carter Hardware where, if you didn't treat the customer right, you surely would not see him again. My father took those same high standards into the arena of national and international business, where the "rules of the road" do not always include such high-mindedness.

An entrepreneur is an individual who risks his time and money to achieve profit. And my father was not just an entrepreneur. As Builders Emporium demonstrated, he was a visionary. No one else had the foresight to innovate as he did—with the size of the store, the broad mix of offerings, the idea of bringing supermarket-style shopping to the hardware industry, and even the idea of expanding a small store into something huge. It is frequently said that business success boils down to finding a need and filling it. My father's genius for recognizing opportunity and his mental framework, which said, "Do it ... *right now,*" meant that he not only recognized the trends but capitalized on them.

The next logical step with Builders Emporium would have been to franchise it. My father certainly considered the idea of bringing the business to other cities, but instead he chose to sell the store. He may well have noticed that the demographic trends were changing, that the do-it-yourself era might have peaked for the foreseeable future. For whatever reason, he made up his mind to sell. The new owners indeed franchised Builders Emporium around the country.

When he sold the store, Victor began his third sabbatical. Again he took his time and thought long and hard about which direction to explore next. This third hiatus gave him more time to spend with my mother and me, and more mental space in which to conceive his business plan, one that would be totally unlike anything he had done before.

At the same time that he was creating financial abundance for the Carter family, he was also working extremely hard in a different role—that of philanthropist and organizer of philanthropic ventures. My father gave back to the community in extraordinary measure. Not only did he contribute large sums of money to the medical, religious, communal, educational, cultural, and international causes close to his heart, but he also brought his genius for organizing and planning to the organizations he inevitably led.

12

Thinking About Money

MY FATHER LOVED TO SAY, "Money's nothing. It's just a piece of paper. It's something that keeps track of our IOUs, and that I did this for you, and you did this for me. ... We invest it with meaning. In and of itself, intrinsically, it's absolutely nothing. It's what you can do with it that matters."

My father's sense that money wasn't the alpha and omega of life freed him from the obligation to sit at his desk constantly and live a narrow, money-oriented life. Instead, he was able to use money as a means of a life well lived. He loved his black Cadillac convertibles, which he would trade in every few years because he drove them so intensely. And he was exceptionally generous to my mother, to me, and to everyone in his life. In addition, his attitude about money allowed him to take the sabbatical years between Carter Hardware and Vimcar, between Vimcar and Builders Emporium, and then again after he sold Builders Emporium. In the years after he completed his last major business endeavor, Republic Pictures, my father did not devote his life merely to increasing his wealth, although that certainly occurred. Instead, he was very happy to travel the world with my mother, going on annual cruises of four months or longer, visiting Israel several times a year, and traveling throughout the country.

When my father traveled, he had the gift of being able to shut down the side of him that worried about business. Except for a few minutes a day when he was communicating with his office, business did not exist for him when he was cruising, traveling to Israel, or otherwise engaged in the pursuit of relaxation. He certainly checked in with his office daily, and his ship-to-shore phone bill rivaled the cost of other passengers' cruises. Once he got off the phone, though, he had the marvelous ability to enjoy himself and to enjoy the life that his wealth permitted our family. My father loved to spend time alone with my mother and with me, and when he was with us, he truly was *with* us.

People whose lives were measured just in terms of their net worth or their company's balance sheet were different from my father. Those committed to financial success and little else were, in my father's opinion, missing the boat, literally. How many of his peers, even those who were wealthier, would have taken a four-month cruise with their spouses? How many of them would have done so every year? How many of them could have "turned off" the business mechanism in their minds so that they could enjoy and be fully present with those they loved?

Was he a tough businessman, a shrewd negotiator, a formidable opponent? Ask anyone who ever did business with him. He knew and loved the art of the deal. Yet, as I said, he also felt that if you made a deal with someone, everyone had to go away happy. My father was a master of the art of win/win. He counted his success in terms of how well he knew the merchandise, how quickly he could serve the customer, and whether he could provide a price that was considerably better than those of any of his competitors. This was certainly his approach at Carter Hardware, and he carried that philosophy over into Builders Emporium and every business venture he undertook. He never thought in terms of "I've gotta make money" or "I've gotta beat the other guy." He simply thought in terms of doing the best job possible.

For him, sales and entrepreneurship were extremely creative processes. He believed deeply in whatever he was doing—and he was always "in the moment," whether he was helping people

94

build barbecues in their backyards at Builders Emporium or campaigning for Israel Bonds. Whatever he believed in, he believed in all the way, and if he was committed, he could sell that idea to anyone.

My father had a phrase that reflected his worldview: "*And then some!*" This phrase connoted his ideas about giving, commitment, and responsibility. It meant that you would use every ounce of your energy and even after that find some more as you sought to achieve a worthy goal. He also had a philosophical approach to setbacks of any kind: "This too shall pass." He never let any situation overly disturb him.

Clearly, there is a paradox here. He was a man who was not intrinsically committed to the idea of making money, but who went out and made so much. The resolution of that paradox, in my mind, is that he knew he would always be successful. Consequently, he was able to devote all of his time to doing the things that created success without succumbing to self-doubt or confusion. He always knew where he was going in life.

My father was fascinated by the human mind and deeply interested in people. He was always trying to understand them, especially those who worked for him, so that he could better motivate them or bring out the best in them. At one point he became fascinated with the idea that "things are *what* they are because of *where* they are." The psychologist who gave him this notion had drawn an apple and depicted one person on one side of the apple and another person on the other side. My father loved the idea that people see things from their perspective because of where they are in life. For a supposedly hard-headed businessman, he did have a philosophical turn of mind. He knew that the higher one's perspective, the greater one's vision. For Victor, taking the high road also meant seeing things from the most ethically elevated perspective. He did not believe that an individual had to scuttle his values in order to succeed in business.

The charitable endeavors my father undertook in his lifetime were vast, ranging from the medical to the educational, from the scientific to the communal and the cultural aspects of life. The range of his philanthropy reflected the great breadth of his remarkable interests and the power of his mind. Any organization fortunate enough to have Victor M. Carter involved was assured of not just a substantial financial contribution but a level of energy, responsiveness, and stick-to-it-iveness that would transform that organization.

13

Giving Back

LIKE MANY SUCCESSFUL INDIVIDUALS, my father was drawn to philanthropy for a variety of reasons. The example both his parents set guided him throughout his life. Certainly, the frustration that he could do nothing to save Bobby's life caused him to find ways to ease the suffering of others. His own upbringing in prerevolutionary Russia, where he saw examples of great human courage and enormous suffering and tragedy, also sensitized him to the needs of others. Charitable giving was deeply embedded in my father's roots, both as a Carter and as a Jew.

Jews have a concept called *tikkun olam,* which means "repairing the world." The idea is that the world is imperfect and needs mending, and it is the job of each of us to contribute, in our own way, to improve the lot of our fellow man. My father combined a generous nature with his "right now" mentality of getting things done and his unique gift for organizing. With all of these elements at work in his personality, it is little wonder that he evolved into an extraordinarily dynamic philanthropist, benefactor, and leader—not just in his home city of Los Angeles but on three continents.

In my father's office in West Los Angeles are two index-card containers, each a foot long. They don't look like anything special until you open them up and see what they contain. These two feet of index cards record the story of his charitable giving over half a century. Hundreds and perhaps even thousands of organizations of every stripe are represented. These include Jewish organizations, charities related to medical research, institutions in Israel, and groups that oppose bias because of race, religion, or sexual orientation. My father was an extraordinarily generous man, and if all he had accomplished in terms of philanthropy were the donations in these two index-card containers, as the Passover expression says, *dayenu*—it would have been enough. Every organization he touched was transformed by his energy, generosity, and the way he persuaded others to come on board.

The stories about what he accomplished are endless. Most of them are untold and will never be told, because my father never sought to be honored for doing the right thing. He was not the kind of person who did things because he wanted the recognition. He did things because they needed to be done. He often told me that if you wanted to get people to do things, you had to give them *cavod*—honor, respect, recognition. And yet he never sought it for himself.

As a boy in Russia, my father attended *cheder*—Jewish school—with its emphasis on a Talmudic education. One of the most important principles of Judaism is the concept of *tzedakah,* often translated as "charity," but the word means much more. The root of the Hebrew word *tzedakah* is *tzedek,* meaning justice or righteousness. In other words, the Torah commands Jews to give charity not because they may feel themselves in a charitable mood, but instead because it is the just and right thing to do.

My father's attitude toward his communal and charitable endeavors was deeply rooted in this notion. Helping others who were poor or unable to afford health care, or lacking the rights and dignity to which all human beings are entitled, was not just due to his charitable feelings, but rather a matter deeply rooted in basic concepts of right and wrong.

My father's first major foray into *tzedakah* came with the City of Hope, the Southern California hospital complex founded by my grandfather Mark and other leading Jewish businessmen in the early part of the twentieth century. At the time, one of the major health concerns of immigrants to the United States was

Victor with former first lady Eleanor Roosevelt at the City of Hope, 1950.

tuberculosis. Crowded, poorly ventilated tenements were breeding grounds for TB, which tragically shortened the lives of countless immigrants of every nationality, and there were few, if any, settings in which a poor person could receive treatment for tuberculosis.

At the same time, discrimination kept many Jews from being admitted to those hospitals that did treat TB. My grandfather Mark and his friends and business associates recognized this and decided to do something about it. What they did was to create the City of Hope, which began as a tuberculosis treatment center in Duarte, California, for those Jews who either could not afford treatment or could not find admission to hospitals in their regions.

By the 1940s, my father had become active in City of Hope affairs, and he served as chairman of the board of that organization from 1949 to 1957. He brought a sense of energy and fun to fundraising for the City of Hope, which remains one of the central pillars of philanthropy in Los Angeles. Today the City of Hope is a nonsectarian institution, serving cancer patients and performing research. It is also one of the most modern major hospital complexes in the United States. When the City of Hope began, its facilities consisted of nothing more than two tents. The patients and doctors came first; permanent buildings came later.

Under my father's direction, the City of Hope launched a support organization called the Sportsman's Club, which provided evenings of entertainment for Angelinos while raising money and recognition for the City of Hope. For example, as a member of the Sportsman's Club, my father started a program called Fight for Lives, which sponsored boxing matches that were also fund-raising evenings for the City of Hope. I remember attending those boxing matches with my father and his

With actor-comedian Bob Hope at the City of Hope.

friends. These were spirited, fun evenings that raised enormous amounts of money.

While chairman of the board of the City of Hope, Victor discovered that the same skills that had brought him so much business success—his ability to create a vision and lead and inspire others to go beyond whatever limits they had imagined for themselves—were just as successful in the world of philanthropy and nonprofits. In addition to serving as chairman of the board of the City of Hope, he was president of the United Jewish Welfare Fund, the Jewish Federation Council, the United Way, the United Crusade, the Japan-America Society, and Israel Bonds.

When my father was the president of an organization, he was deeply involved in every aspect of that organization, bringing his business acumen—and his Rolodex—to determine how best to handle problems. He was not a figurehead; he was a doer. Whatever he took on, he took on with intense dedication. A story in the *Los Angeles Times* on Sunday, July 26, 1987, illustrates the effect he had on the organizations he headed:

PHILANTHROPIST VICTOR CARTER LEADS BY EXAMPLE

In '67, when Carter was the chairman of the annual United Way drive, he raised his own donation from $6,000 to $10,000. Then he heard that other people were giving as much as $25,000 in other cities. So he talked it over with Leonard Firestone, another leading businessman, and they each upped their donations to $25,000 and persuaded ten others to do the same. Today there are $100,000 donors, but the United Way credits Carter, who established a whole new aspect of personal giving in Los Angeles. The United Way gave him the Alexis de Tocqueville Society Award at the Kennedy Center in Washington.

*At the 70th anniversary dinner: back row, left to right, Robin Buckner,
Rich Buckner, Leigh Silverton, Steve Crowley, Sheri Silverton, Jim Weatherford;
front row, Adrea Carter, William Buckner, Victor Carter, Devin Jackson,
Fanya Carter, Katie Buckner, Jack Delchamps.*

The United Way took it a step further—the annual award they give their most dedicated supporter is called the Victor M. Carter Humanitarian Award.

For all the fuss made over my father, he remained unchanged in terms of his personal modesty. His longtime attorney, Hugh Sommers, recounts a story of when the two men were in court, handling a business matter. My father leaned toward Sommers and whispered, "Do you think the judge will let me leave the court at 3:30? I've got to go home and change for a formal dinner. It has to do with Tel Aviv University. It's something I helped out with."

Sommers asked the judge if my father could be excused, and the judge replied in the affirmative. The next morning, Sommers recalls, he read an article in the *Los Angeles Times* that said the dinner, a black-tie affair at which Golda Meir was present, was given in my father's honor, because he had been the principal financial benefactor for that project. Sommers was struck by the fact that my father did not have a particular need to "look good" in front of his own attorney or the judge. If there ever had been a moment when he could have bragged, surely that would have been it.

Many of Victor's good deeds were done without fanfare or publicity. As a case in point, he was visiting a friend in a hospital in Israel where he met a Tanzanian gentleman who told my father of his desire to become a doctor and help people. My father gave him his card and said, "Look me up if I can help you." Years later, the man wrote to my father saying, "I hope you remember me. We met at the hospital in Israel." He needed help getting a visa in order to begin his medical studies in the United States. My father not only helped him get a visa but paid his tuition and living expenses, so that he was able to graduate as a doctor from an American medical school. The Tanzanian went back to his homeland where he practiced medicine for many years. We arranged for this doctor to attend my parents' seventieth wedding anniversary at the Hillcrest Country Club, because we wanted others to know what my father had done for him. The doctor in turn wished to be present to re-state his appreciation for having been able to contribute to the welfare of his country.

Rivian Chaikin, my father's longtime personal assistant, told of the time that United Cerebral Palsy called Victor's office, looking for a donation of perhaps a few hundred dollars toward the purchase of a new van. My father asked how much the van would cost. Around $25,000, was the response. OK, my father said, he would pay for the new van. Rivian says she can still remember the woman screaming with surprise and delight. That was just my father's way—do it, do it to the limit, and do it without any need for recognition or glory.

The link in his mind between charity and justice was most clearly evident in his relations with Japanese-Americans during and after World War II, and with the African-American community during the Civil Rights era. My father first came in contact with Japanese-Americans while working at Carter Hardware back in the 1920s. He was fascinated by their language and culture, and he took an extended trip to Japan in 1937, to build up business contacts in that nation. He was outraged by the segregation of Japanese-Americans into internment camps during World War II, and he fought hard to keep those Japanese-Americans he knew from internment or from losing their homes and businesses. After the war, my father conspicuously employed Japanese-Americans at Vimcar, to make the point to the rest of the business world that discrimination was intolerable. He was also instrumental in re-establishing the Japanese banks of California, and he helped many Japanese-Americans recover income and bonds that had been appropriated by the government from those banks.

Victor as Goodwill Ambassador to Japan, with Adrea (right).

In 1968, the Emperor of Japan decorated my father with the Order of the Sacred Treasure. This award is rarely presented to non-Japanese citizens and had never before been given to anyone under the age of seventy. Victor was fifty-nine at the time. He was then president of the Japan-America Society. At the same time, he was also the head of the Los Angeles Jewish Federation Council and the United Way and honorary chairman of the Los Angeles Committee of Israel Bonds. He also helped found the Japanese Philharmonic Orchestra, the only Japanese orchestra outside of Japan.

One small, entertaining sidelight of my father's involvement with the Japanese: a letter in his files from the Consul General of Japan in Los Angeles, dated October 18, 1974, thanking him for extending courtesies to the Japanese Minister of State when he spent two days in Los Angeles on his way to Washington. Many Japanese are golf-crazy, and the Minister of State was among them. The Consul General wrote, "On October 11, His Excellency expressed a desire to play a round of golf, and, since the Hillcrest Country Club is located so conveniently near the Century Plaza Hotel where the party stayed, you kindly made special arrangements for luncheon and golf at the club for His Excellency. ... Needless to say, His Excellency enjoyed himself thoroughly and was deeply grateful for the many courtesies extended him by the Hillcrest management."

My father was also deeply involved in the struggle for civil rights in this country. He became a friend and leading supporter of both Martin Luther King Jr. and Medgar Evers, the head of the NAACP in Mississippi. My father's concern for African-Americans was rooted in his own experience as a Jew and therefore a second-class citizen in pre-revolutionary Russia. When Dr. King needed buses to bring supporters from Los Angeles to the nation's capitol for the Poor Persons March on Washington, my father paid for those buses. The nature of the bond between Dr. King and my father is captured beautifully in the way the civil rights leader inscribed a copy of his 1963 book, *Strength to Love*, to my parents:

> To my friends Mr. and Mrs. Victor Carter,
> in appreciation for your deep humanitarian concern,
> your genuine goodwill, and your unswerving devotion
> to the cause of freedom and justice.
> — Martin Luther King

When Evers, another leading civil rights advocate in the early 1960s, was gunned down in his driveway by white supremacists, my father gathered at our home a group of Los Angeles civic leaders and celebrities, including Marlon Brando and Eartha Kitt. At that meeting, Victor undertook to pay for the college educations of Evers' children. According to Rivian, my father's secretary, Evers' children frequently called him for advice as they made their way in their early adult years. After the Watts riots of 1965, my father helped found Operation Bootstrap, which brought jobs and other forms of assistance to the inner city with the goal of creating economic self-sufficiency for its residents.

Victor's political accomplishments were also legion, if generally behind the scenes. On a national level, he was an advisor to President Lyndon Johnson. In Los Angeles, he served with distinction on the Harbor Commission, the Southern California Rapid Transit District Board of Directors, and the Water and Power Commission. And the crowning achievement of his commitment to racial equality took place when Mayor Sam Yorty of Los Angeles appointed him head of the Fire Commission. At the time, the L.A. Fire Department was segregated—no blacks were permitted to work in firehouses in predominantly white neighborhoods. My father single-handedly brought about the end of

Victor (third from left) receiving an award for his work on the Los Angeles Fire Commission, 1950.

THE PORT OF LOS ANGELES

REPORTER

News of and for the Employees of the City of Los Angeles Harbor Department PREPARED BY THE PUBLIC RELATIONS DIVISION

VOL. 2, NO. 1   JANUARY 1968

MAYOR SAM YORTY, LEFT, LOOKS ON AS VICTOR M. CARTER, center, is sworn in as a member of the Los Angeles Board of Harbor Commissioners by City Clerk Walter C. Thiel. Carter, prominent businessman and philanthropist, was recently appointed to the post by the Mayor and confirmed by the City Council.

Carter Appointed To Harbor Commission

When Victor Carter was appointed to the Harbor Commission last December 6, he reached another milestone in a varied and distinguished career of public service.

A semi-retired Los Angeles businessman and philanthropist, he was named by Mayor Sam Yorty to replace the late Pietro Di Carlo. Carter's term on the board will expire July 1, 1969.

The new commissioner is a retired board chairman of Republic Corp. of Beverly Hills. Active also in the manufacture and distribution of building materials, he founded Builder's Emporium.

His civic and philanthropic pursuits include the United Crusade, which he headed this year, and the City of Hope, which he led as board president for eight years.

Carter, 57, is also a director of the Los Angeles Chamber of Commerce and the Los Angeles World Affairs Council. In addition, he is affiliated with the Japan-America Council and the Interracial Council for Business Opportunities.

He was a member of the Board of Fire Commissioners for six years and served as president of that body in 1957 and 1958.

With Carter's addition, the Board of Harbor Commissioners is as follows: Gordon G. MacLean, President; Taul Watanabe, vice president; and members George D. Watson, Robert A. Day and Carter.

Bowling Teams Roll On 'n On 'n On

Bouncing balls and tumbling ten pins, the bowling teams strike forward with plenty of weeks to spare.

Christmas hams and turkeys for best scores were awarded to the following: Betty Munoz, Ruth Gehrts, Alvera Brodt, Barbara Scott, Mike Mikkelson, Jess Martinez, Dick Jackson and Harry Miller.

Leading the league of 14 teams is "Lucky Thirteen" skippered by John Herrera, Engineering. The crew consists of Gloria Radmilovich, Ron Lopez, Bonnie and John Phillips.

Captains of the other teams are Ruth Gehrts, Pete Squires, Rose Kilgore, Jess Martinez, Wayne Tennant, John Smith, Carmen DiMeglio, Bonnie Orlando, Alvera Brodt, Harry Harless, Ken Valdez, Nelson Cole and Henry Munoz.

President of the league, which has been in existence since 1960, is Harry Miller, Legal. Vice president is Jim Aarhus, Engineering, and secretary, Bonnie Orlando.

Discount Tickets

Tickets at a discount rate are available to All City Employee Association members for the following exciting attractions:

NBC Color City TV Studio Tour; Wax Museum; Ivar Theater, Paul Goldin, E.S.P.; Palm Springs Aerial Tramway; Lakers and Kings games; Sea World; Marineland of the Pacific; Magic Kingdom membership cards (Disneyland); Antique show and sale, Long Beach Municipal Auditorium, Jan. 25–26.

Joerline Miralles (Legal - Ext. 215) suggests one person in each division draw up a list of those interested in tickets. The lists should then be turned over to Joerline. When applying, the employee should list his name, address and zip code. Only members of the All City Employee Association are eligible to participate.

Ethel and Tom Bradley with Adrea and Victor Carter.

segregation in the L.A. Fire Department, over the strong resistance of the old-line bigots who wanted to preserve the status quo.

In recognition of his devotion to the welfare of Los Angeles firefighters and his successful efforts at desegregating the Los Angeles Fire Department, a detachment of firefighters, in dress uniform, was present at my father's funeral, to pay their final respects. In addition, the *Wave*, one of the leading African-American publications in Los Angeles at the time of my father's death, devoted its front page to his obituary. The article declared that Victor M. Carter had done more for the black community of Los Angeles than any black leader.

My father first met the future mayor of Los Angeles, Tom Bradley, when Bradley was campaigning during the primary and came to him seeking financial support. Victor explained that he was already committed to the campaign of another Democratic candidate, Tom Reddin. Bradley took the news with surprising calm, which impressed my father. Instead of expressing disappointment, Bradley asked whether he might count on my father's support should Bradley win the primary. My father, an outstanding judge of character, was struck by the coolness and courage Bradley displayed in making the request; he agreed to support Bradley should he win the party's nomination, which, of course, he did.

It's also possible that my father believed it was time for Los Angeles to have an African-American mayor, and Bradley, with his sterling record as a police officer and his outstanding reputation in Los Angeles civic life, was an excellent candidate in my father's eyes. The two men became close friends, so much so that when my father celebrated his eightieth birthday, Bradley, then frail, attended the party and shook my father's hand with tears in his eyes. The two men were devoted to each other throughout their lives.

When my father passed away in March 2004, the head of the Urban League, John Mack, offered this perspective: "He was a great champion of human rights, civil rights, and a great human being. He truly cared about all people, no matter who they were. He was extremely generous financially, but he did more than write a check. He became personally involved and worked hard to build bridges of mutual respect and understanding. Victor was a leader for all seasons and one of a kind."[1]

From the two feet of index cards representing the thousands of organizations to which he made annual and often quite sizable donations, to his service to the Jewish, Japanese-American, and African-American communities, my father made an indelible mark not only on the city but also on the world. *Los Angeles Magazine*, in a June 1985 cover story on the city's Jewish community, named my father one of the ten leading members of that community. Herb Gelfand, a leading builder and philanthropist in Los Angeles, says that my father set a powerful example for the men of Gelfand's generation. Victor inspired them, Gelfand says, to shoulder philanthropic responsibilities and to give generously of their time and resources. So my father's dedication to his community, his religion, and his world is echoed in the acts of younger philanthropists, a fact that would please him greatly.

My father's activities in the State of Israel, charitable and business related, are so numerous and varied that they deserve their own chapter.

---

1. "Services Held for Victor M. Carter," *Wave Community Newspapers*, March 31, 2004, p. 1

Victor and Adrea with President Harry S. Truman.

Adrea and Victor with Vice President Hubert Humphrey and his wife, Muriel.

With President Richard Nixon.

Victor and Adrea with President Ronald Reagan.

With Nancy Reagan.

With President Bill Clinton.

Victor (center) with Governor Goodwin Knight of California (left) and legendary comedian Jack Benny.

With Governor Pat Brown of California.

With Ronald Reagan, former governor of California.

Fanya, Victor and Adrea with Los Angeles Mayor Sam Yorty.

Victor and Adrea with Los Angeles Mayor Tom Bradley.

The Carters with Dr. Martin Luther King Jr.

With the Dalai Lama: Fanya Carter, husband Jack Delchamps, Victor Carter (in background, far right).

*Victor and Adrea Carter flanking singer Eartha Kitt and actor Marlon Brando;
the occasion was a fund-raising effort for the education of the children of slain
civil rights leader Medgar Evers.*

Victor (left) and Adrea (far right) with television and film star Jackie Gleason.

Victor and Adrea with film stars Elizabeth Taylor and Richard Burton.

With actress Jayne Mansfield.

Adrea and Victor with Bob Hope.

Author Fanya Carter with Marlon Brando.

14

In the Land of Israel

LIKE MANY JEWS, my father first became interested in Zionism at the end of World War II. He shared the belief—and the dream—that Jews should have their own homeland, so as to prevent the possibility of a recurrence of the Nazi Holocaust. From 1948 on, he was deeply involved with the State of Israel on many levels, a friend and advisor to every prime minister from the founding of the country until his death.

He was deeply committed to nurturing the business life of the country, sharing his knowledge, his contacts, and his wealth with the creators of the new state. On a charitable level, he was involved in the founding of Tel Aviv University and other educational institutions and provided parks and tennis courts for Israel's youth. He was also chairman of the board of Israel's largest private investment holding company, which controlled, by 1967, more than $250 million of the country's economy. It is not an exaggeration to say that my father was as great a friend to the State of Israel as anyone in its first fifty years.

When Israel was founded, it needed to know how to train the generation of engineers, technicians, specialists and business-people who could manage the country's business and scientific growth. Victor was adept in all of these areas and lent a huge amount of technical assistance to the young nation. His role in the founding of Tel Aviv University was an outgrowth of a conversation with then Israeli Prime Minister Golda Meir. The prime minister told my father that Israel needed an institution to provide technical training, and my father helped that institution open its doors by making a large donation and persuading many others to do likewise. While he was chairman of the board of governors of Tel Aviv University from 1970 to 1976, a job he took on at Golda Meir's request, his first task was to build the Joseph Meirhoff Technical High School near the university. Victor told the *Jerusalem Post* in 1984, "If technical training is not increased, then it will be a mistake for which Israel will pay dearly. Nothing must be spared in order to educate the right people for the right kind of industry."

My father's role as chairman of the Tel Aviv University board of governors required him to travel to Israel at least five times a year. While he was chairman, the university grew to 15,000 students and received critical acclaim from individuals such as world-renowned physicist Edward Teller, who said that "Tel Aviv University ranks higher than the best universities in the United States."

Victor's involvement in Israeli affairs was not limited to educational matters. He served on the executive boards of Israel Discount Banks and Klal Industries, one of Israel's largest conglomerates. He was also deeply involved with Teva, the Israeli pharmaceutical company. My father met the founder of Teva, Eli Hurwitz, early on and was so impressed that he purchased a large block of stock. My father introduced Teva to the world's leading businesspeople and government officials, and Teva became one of the largest and most successful companies of its kind. Today, Teva is the largest producer of generic drugs in the world. The investment that Victor made in Teva turned out to be one of his most financially astute decisions, multiplying itself many, many times over. Truly, my father was able, as the expression goes, to do well by doing good.

The Six Day War in 1967 was a high point in my father's support for the State of Israel. He convened a huge assembly of the Los Angeles Jewish community at the Hollywood Bowl and raised phenomenal amounts of money for Israel during a war that many people feared would erase that nation from the map.

Victor also chaired the Israel Economic Development Conference. He traveled all over Europe, the United States, and South America to visit leading Jewish businesspeople and persuade them to invest in and do business with the State of Israel. I accompanied him on some of those trips, and it was always awe-inspiring to watch my father in action. The Israel Economic Development Conference played a large role in getting American businesses to invest $200 million in Israel. As a chairman of the Economic Development Conference, Victor was instrumental in helping sixty-seven of *Fortune's* top five hundred Israeli businesses.

My father was frequently honored for his efforts to support Israel. He received hundreds of plaques recognizing those efforts. My parents never knew what to do with all those plaques from Jewish organizations large and small. Victor was not the type to create huge monuments to himself. Finally they did hang several dozen—perhaps one percent of all he received—in a rarely visited back hall. My father did not really care much for plaques—they represented past achievements, and he was interested in the present and the future. What mattered most to him was what he could do *right now*.

My father somehow managed to hold his legendary impatience in check when he and my mother set out to build a home for themselves in Israel, a gorgeous penthouse apartment on top of the Moriah Hotel in downtown Jerusalem. From that penthouse they enjoyed sweeping views of the Old City, the Dome of the Rock, and the hills surrounding Jerusalem. But building in Israel is not like building in North America. Work happens slowly and projects move forward only sporadically. It took the workers five years to complete that apartment, and yet my father never lost his patience, or his faith in the project.

I remember traveling with them to Israel to find out how the construction was coming along. Whatever my father asked, the answer was always, "No problem, Mr. Carter!" He was able to tolerate the delay only because he loved Israel so much. I can't imagine that a man who did not suffer fools gladly would have exercised the same patience had those delays happened back in the United States.

My parents were close with all of the leaders of Israel, especially prime ministers Golda Meir, Yitzhak Rabin, Shimon Perez, and Menachem Begin, and the legendary mayor of Jerusalem, Teddy Kollek. Victor's friendships and contacts elsewhere in the Israeli government are too numerous to list. I really think my parents became friends with these people not because my father enjoyed rubbing shoulders with celebrities or the powerful but the other way around: The Israeli leadership admired *him* so much and they needed and wanted so much from him that they drew him into *their* circle.

His voluminous correspondence files represented a who's who of Israeli and other world leaders—Winston Churchill among them—going back decades. My father had what Israel needed— the knowledge base necessary to help build the country, the contacts with other business leaders in the United States and around the world, and the financial wherewithal to make multimillion-dollar donations. But I believe that the leaders of Israel spent so much time with my father, socializing with him and my mother on countless occasions, either at my parents' apartment at the Moriah or in their own homes, simply because my parents were so much fun to be with. They were always the life of any party they attended, and this was just as true when they were with the top echelon of Israeli society as when they were anywhere else.

Adrea and Victor with Golda Meir.

My father and Golda Meir shared a deep bond of friendship. Back then, the Israeli government ran on extraordinarily informal terms—the top leaders would literally meet in Golda Meir's kitchen, over coffee, trying to figure out how to solve Israel's numerous problems. On many occasions, my father attended meetings of the "Kitchen Cabinet" and shared his ideas about how to create Israel's future. My father loved this courageous woman who made so many brave decisions. A scene in the play *Golda* demonstrates her decisiveness during the Yom Kippur War in 1973, when Egypt caught Israel by surprise and nearly eradicated the Jewish state. The Russians had announced that they were going to bomb Israel if the prime minister did not take a certain action; she determined, somehow, that they were bluffing, and she called their bluff. That steadfastness and courage inspired the men who served under her to love, admire and respect her. That certainly represents how my father felt about her.

The effects of my father's humanitarianism are evident throughout Israel, whether it is the symphony orchestra that he founded for Tel Aviv University, the technical high school mentioned earlier, or any of the countless playgrounds, parks, hospitals, community centers, and other institutions he underwrote. There's a funny story about Teddy Kollek, the mayor of Jerusalem, who was creating a Noah's Ark animal park for the children of Jerusalem. Supporters could make a donation and receive a plaque dedicating an animal. For two million dollars, for example, you got the hippopotamus, and for twenty-five thousand dollars, you got, say, an owl or some other small creature. Teddy was trying to persuade my father, then in his eighties, to underwrite the largest, most expensive animal, a mythical elephant-giraffe figure designed by the artist Niki de Sainte Falle. Naturally, my father agreed to do so.

When he was ninety and my mother was eighty-nine, my parents, a team of caregivers, my husband, Jack, and I flew to Israel for my parents' last trip there. We went to attend the dedication of the Tel Aviv University Philharmonic, for which my father was the principal benefactor.

My father's role as an unofficial ambassador for Israel brought him into contact with leaders around the globe. He never refrained from speaking his mind when he was in contact with them, no matter who they were or how important they were. A letter in his files to President Habib Bourguiba of Tunisia testifies to this fact. Bourguiba evidently had spoken out against the annihilation of the State of Israel, and my father's strong feelings shine through this letter:

> June 4, 1965
> President Habib Bourguiba
> Tunis, Tunisia

Your Excellency:

Your public rejection of the concept of annihilation has come at a most welcome time.

The past year has seen one issue after another in the Middle East, mishandled with the same stereotyped blindness and bitterness and with the same lack of recognition of the realities of the world in which we live.

Now, Sir, you have said what we have long dreamed of hearing an Arab leader say one day; that the Arab world does not live in a vacuum and that the Arab-Israel dispute is capable of solution and indeed its solution is necessary if the Arab Peoples are to advance.

Please do not consider me presumptuous in congratulating you on the statesmanship of your approach, on your courage and on your candor, which I feel sure must bring us much closer to the pacification of this important area of the world, in which two great historic Peoples must learn to live in harmony.

Sincerely,
Victor M. Carter
President and Chairman of the Board

The fact that the person my father was addressing in such strong terms was the leader of a nation was of no consequence. He had an opinion to share, and no one was going to keep him from speaking his mind!

In addition to Jewish causes, my father also contributed generously to other groups that lived in the land of Israel. The Jewish State, of course, contains not only Jews; it contains Christians, Moslems, and a large population of Druze, Arab Christians who are friendly to the State of Israel. On one trip in 1965, my father came in contact with the leadership of the Druze community in Acco. One of those leaders wrote a charming letter to my father: "You are a noble person," the judge wrote. "I promised my son Kamel to give your important help (sic) for the school building which contains sixteen rooms and is supposed to collect four hundred pupils. Till now we have finished about six rooms and we are still going to finish the rest. So we hope that you will send us your valuable aid for that vital and human project in order to buy the necessary materials like cement, iron, and wood as soon as possible."

Another Druze leader, Salman Tarif, the Kaddi of the Druze community, wrote to my father: "There are many miles between America and Israel, but hearts know no distance. All the respect and consideration to Your Honor. The sheikhs and the poor and the family convey their salutations to Your Honor."

They saw Victor Carter for the leader he truly was.

Yet the most satisfying of my father's efforts in Israel took place far from the limelight. One of his favorite charitable efforts in that country was Project Renewal, which helped low-income residents of Jerusalem. A young man from Musrar, a poor neighborhood in the city, asked my father to guarantee his bond with a bank so that he could become a building contractor. My father did so, and according to the *Jerusalem Post*, years later the young man did the same thing for another resident in his neighborhood who was trying to get started in the building business. My father always preferred to help individuals by "teaching them to fish" rather than catching the fish for them, and in so doing he changed lives and transformed communities.

Victor received a gold medal from Israeli Prime Minister Levi Eshkol in 1968 for his service to the Economic Conference, and he later was awarded an honorary doctorate from Tel Aviv University because of his support for that institution. The most remarkable thing about him was not the breadth of his activities or the depth of his support. It was in his commitment to *results*. He wanted to make things happen, regardless of who got the credit. His essential humanity and modesty consistently radiated through all of his efforts—political, financial, business, educational, or communitarian. His modesty about his own remarkable achievements is evident in a story that his longtime secretary Rivian told.

At some point, Rivian found a picture in a corner of his office showing my father with Golda Meir. She asked whether he wanted her to put it in a nice frame and display it prominently in the office.

Truly surprised by the question, my father turned to her and asked, "Who on earth would care about that?"

First Israeli Prime Minister David Ben-Gurion with the Carters and granddaughters Robin Buckner and Sheri Silverton (next to Victor, right).

With Israeli General Moshe Dayan.

From left, author Fanya Carter; Israeli Foreign Minister Abba Eben; Sheri and Leigh Silverton; Victor Carter.

Victor (standing, right) with Israeli Prime Minister Golda Meir (second from left) at Israel Bonds event.

Victor (center) with Golda Meir.

Adrea and Victor with Israeli Prime Minister Yitzhak Rabin (second from left).

Victor and Adrea in Tel Aviv. Victor was being honored for his years of service as President of Tel Aviv University.

15

The Republic Corporation

WHILE MY FATHER WAS SO DEEPLY INVOLVED with charitable and civic responsibilities, in Los Angeles, in Israel, and in Japan, he managed nonetheless to use his time and energy to create one more chapter in his professional life. The one-time clerk at Carter Hardware now became the CEO of a corporation traded on the New York Stock Exchange.

During the mid-1950s my father became aware of the desirability of owning a controlling interest in Republic Pictures. A number of factors made the company appealing to him. Living in Los Angeles, he was well aware of the financial success that could come from owning assets in the film and television industry. Television was just taking off, and the need for sound stages and studio space was growing rapidly. The real estate controlled by Republic was also attractive to my father. Republic's studios were located on Radford Street in Studio City in the San Fernando Valley, where CBS Studio Center stands today. In addition, a businessman like my father knew how to capitalize on the benefits that accrued from owning a company traded on the New York Stock Exchange.

Victor never did anything in business for one reason alone. When he saw an opportunity, he saw every aspect of it, all the layers and possibilities. With Republic, he realized that he could hire out the sound stages to the TV networks, benefit from the value of the real estate, *and* reap the rewards of owning a NYSE-listed company.

After his successful experience in retail at Builders Emporium, he decided that he wanted to return to the manufacture and distribution of hardware items, an area of business with which he had had enormous success at Vimcar. In order to own the enormous, nationwide manufacturing concerns that interested him, he needed an enterprise large enough to be traded on the New York Stock Exchange to serve as a holding company for such manufacturers. Republic Pictures, my father astutely realized, could serve this additional purpose.

Until Victor came along, Republic was the creation and plaything of Herbert Yates, who started his career as a salesman for tobacco companies. When World War I began, Yates entered the movie industry. By the 1930s, he had created Republic Pictures out of the remains of three smaller, struggling Hollywood production companies located on Gower Street, which was known in the industry in those days as Gower Gulch or Poverty Row. One of those companies had belonged to the famed Hollywood pioneer Mack Sennett.

Under Yates, Republic produced dozens of B movies— mediocre films destined to serve as the second half of double features in tandem with better movies produced at better studios. Republic also became the number one producer in Hollywood of serials, in the tradition of *The Perils of Pauline*. Republic's highly regarded adventure series included *Jungle Girl, Zane Grey's King of the Royal Mounted, Adventures of Captain Marvel*, and *Radar Men from the Moon*. The studio occasionally came through with truly great movies such as Orson Welles' *Macbeth*, in 1948, and John Ford's *The Quiet Man*, in 1952.

By the mid-1950s, however, Republic's stockholders had become increasingly dissatisfied with Yates, for two reasons. First, he refused to allow any of Republic's movies to be broadcast on television, a medium he considered a fad. He did not want

Republic to be associated in any way with the small screen. The second reason was the favoritism Yates displayed toward his wife, Vera Ralston, a Czechoslovakian ice skating star turned Hollywood actress.

Ralston, also known as Vera Hruba Ralston, appeared for her husband in such financially unsuccessful films as *Fair Wind to Java*, *The Man Who Died Twice*, *Gunfire at Indian Gap*, and *Hoodlum Empire*. Indeed, between 1941 and 1958, Vera Ralston appeared in twenty-six movies. By the late 1950s, when my father turned his attention to Republic Pictures, the stock price was deeply depressed and the company was in serious financial trouble. Victor made a deal with Yates to purchase a controlling bloc of Republic Pictures stock. With large corporations, one individual does not have to own more than half of the shares to have control over the direction of the business. Often, as little as ten percent of the outstanding shares of a corporation provides control. My father was suddenly the CEO of a NYSE-traded company. The newest phase of his kaleidoscopically shifting career had begun.

Anyone who thought that he had purchased Republic solely so that he could become a film mogul was swiftly disabused of that idea. He did rent out Republic's facilities for television production, but there were no "Victor M. Carter productions." Instead, his first act, in his first week of running Republic, was to cease all moviemaking. At the time, Vera Ralston was in London with actor Forrest Tucker, making a movie. Victor sent word to London to stop all production on the film immediately. Those involved, including Tucker and Ralston, were given a week to return to Los Angeles at the expense of the studio. If they lingered in London one day longer, they would have to find—and pay for—their own way home.

Victor then changed the name of the company from Republic Pictures to the Republic Corporation. The new Republic went out of the moviemaking business altogether and became a hardware company. He was now able to purchase and run larger industrial enterprises under the auspices of Republic Corporation, including Gaffers and Sattler, which produced gas ranges and stoves, and Pioneer Heating and Air Conditioning.

There was also money to be made from Republic's moviemaking assets. Republic's studios offered a great deal of value to the television industry that Herbert Yates had scorned. My father had recognized the promise of television from its earliest days and was the first in his neighborhood to own a television set. He now entered into a "four wall lease" with CBS Television and the Seven Arts production company, leasing Republic's shuttered moviemaking facilities for TV production. Republic converted its sound stage into a "swing stage," a revolving platform on which more than one scene could be set.

It is expensive and time-consuming to shoot a scene and then strike the set and replace it with the set for the next scene, while highly paid actors and actresses idle in their trailers. My father's swing stage allowed three or four different sets to "swing" into position as necessary, which cut production costs drastically. Among the programs that benefited from this approach was CBS's hit series *Gunsmoke*.

Victor also had some old Republic Pictures business to take care of. At one point, he received a communication from the attorney for John Wayne to the effect that the Republic Corporation, as the successor to Republic Pictures, owed the great Western actor a huge amount of money. It seems that Herbert Yates and John Wayne had met one day at a bar across the street from the studio and signed a contract on a cocktail napkin—Wayne would perform in four pictures for a fee of

$350,000 a picture plus ten percent of the gross of each movie. The men might have struck their deal in a bar, but the contract was valid, and it was up to my father now to make good on Yates' promise.

As it turned out, the four pictures that Wayne made for Yates were all successful, both commercially and critically: *The Sands of Iwo Jima*, *The Fighting Kentuckian* (also starring Vera Ralston!), *The Angel and the Badman*, and *The Wake of the Red Witch*. So my father now found himself on the opposite side of a dispute with none other than John Wayne. He chose to settle the dispute instead of allowing it to fester and turn into a lawsuit.

Victor's approach toward confrontation was never to shy away from it. He was a tough-minded negotiator. If an issue appeared to be headed for court, however, he always wanted to settle rather than litigate. He did not believe in paying large legal fees and having a dispute drain his time and energy when he could settle it quickly and efficiently. So he made a deal with the Wayne people, and the issue was resolved.

After a few years at the helm of Republic, Victor sold his controlling interest in the company to a group headed by New York real estate investor William Zeckendorf, although Victor remained Republic's CEO. Zeckendorf's real estate interests decreased in value, and he found it necessary to sell his shares of Republic to a triumvirate of New York businessmen with a less than stellar reputation for integrity. They immediately fired my father, ostensibly for cause but in fact so that they could run the company, triggering a legal battle that Victor felt obligated to defend.

The attorney representing the three businessmen was none other than Roy Cohn, who had attained national notoriety as an associate of Senator Joseph McCarthy during his anti-Communist crusades of the 1950s. At one point, the three businessmen won a ruling from a state court judge to remove my father from his office at Republic. One of the trio literally took over Victor's office and used his desk and chair. A federal court overturned the state court ruling, kicking the businessman out and restoring my father to his rightful office—whereupon he opened his desk drawer and found a report from a private detective who had been hired to collect some dirt for the campaign against him. The detective had found my father to be something less than a worthwhile target.

"Unfortunately," the report said, "we weren't able to pin very much on him. He doesn't fool around with girls. He doesn't like boys, either. He doesn't smoke or drink, and he's devoted to his family."

At another point in the legal fight, Cohn scheduled an important court hearing in New York for the day after Victor had returned to Los Angeles, assuming that my father's absence would benefit Cohn's clients. Victor landed in Los Angeles, learned of the hearing scheduled for the next day, and immediately went to the airport to fly back to New York, where he was able to defeat the challenge.

The title of one of Republic's most successful pictures— John Wayne's *The Quiet Man*—could just as easily have applied to my father during the time of his legal battles with Roy Cohn and his three clients. Victor began a slow, carefully orchestrated campaign to buy shares of Republic Pictures, so that he could amass a controlling share of the company for the second time. During this period, he never paid more than $8.50 a share for company stock. He could not announce to the world that he was buying shares, because others would have bid up the price in order to "greenmail" my father (that is, make him pay more for the shares). This also would have brought to the attention of others in the marketplace that Republic was an apt target for takeover. So he worked quietly, using brokers in cities across the country to purchase relatively small amounts of the stock at any given time, buying stock in "street name" instead of his own name so that he would not have to reveal his intentions.

He ended up with a controlling interest in the company for a second time. Through his program of judicious stock-buying, he swiftly accomplished his goal—to recover his position as CEO of Republic. The Securities and Exchange Commission requires that anyone who acquires a certain percentage of a company's stock reveal his holdings in government filings, which become a matter of public record. When the news broke that my father had amassed more than ten percent of Republic's stock, the stock price immediately rose substantially. Investors on Wall Street and across the country knew of my father and had a huge amount of respect for his business acumen. They knew that anything my father touched would turn to gold, and so it would be now with Republic.

This news also led to a proxy fight with Cohn's three clients, the three co-owners of the bloc of Republic stock purchased from Zeckendorf's company. My father could win this battle only with proxies, or permissions from share owners to vote their shares in a particular way, delivered to New York in time for the showdown. This was well before FedEx or other overnight shipping companies. So my father conceived the unusual idea of sending the proxies via air freight, which allowed him to prevail when the votes were counted. The three businessmen were defeated, and control of Republic was now firmly in my father's hands.

By the time he sold his interest in Republic, the stock price had risen from the initial $8.50 he had paid to a remarkable $62 a share. He had parlayed an investment of less than $5 million in Republic Pictures stock into millions of dollars of profit.

Victor Carter had done it again.

I tell this story not just because of what it reveals about my father's business success, but because of what it reveals about his character. This remarkable man was able to bear with dignity the "slings and arrows" that came in the form of Cohn's accusations. He demonstrated great perseverance and dedication by fighting for the soul of the company he ran. He took his licks, met his responsibilities, and emerged triumphant.

16

The Mind of Victor Carter

MY FATHER ACCOMPLISHED SO MUCH in business, philanthropy and civic affairs while at the same time maintaining a storybook marriage to my mother. The simple explanation is that he had an extraordinary mind. The more complex question is how his mind differed from that of his fellow man, and how he could create so much in his long lifetime. Two of the keys to my father's frame of mind are *clarity* and *focus*. He simply saw things more clearly and with greater depth than most other people. He had the ability to think with precision and to act fearlessly once he had absorbed all the facts.

Others might have realized that veterans returning from World War II would want to build a deck in their backyard or add a spare room to their new homes. Yet my father was the only one to match that observation with the decision to take a struggling hardware store in the Valley and turn it into the world's first supermarket for hardware. My father was probably not the only businessman who admired Elie Hurwitz and the other founders of Teva, the Israeli biotechnology company. Yet his clear-thinking mind allowed him to recognize that the people starting this company were, like him, visionaries, men worthy of his financial and intellectual support. He parlayed his intuition about Teva's leaders into one of his largest, most successful, and most enduring investments.

You could even say that my father's clarity extended to his personal life—he was eighteen when he met my mother, Adrea, and he knew immediately that she was the perfect woman for him. A couple of meetings led to a long-lasting marriage. The questions remain—what influenced his mind, how did his mode of thinking develop, and how could he always operate from a place of profound clarity?

The roots of that clear thinking go back to his ancestors in Russia, who were either highly successful in business or devout and learned rabbis. The Kartozhinsky family had a long and noble tradition of rabbinical ordination. As a youth, Victor was exposed to the same kind of Talmudical, highly logical training process in his Jewish education that the men in the family had undergone for centuries. He combined that education with his experience growing up at the feet of three generations of successful businessmen. Along with that, he possessed a genius for mathematics, a wide-ranging curiosity about life, and an expectation of success.

My father's formal education ended when he was still a teenager. He was always hungry to learn—about business, people, politics, and the world. He loved facts. He loved to know precisely what was going on. If you provided solid information, you were his friend. If you fudged and speculated, and tried to pass off your speculation as fact, he lost interest quickly. He subscribed to a number of political and business periodicals—the *Wall Street Journal*, the *Kiplinger Report, U.S. News and World Report, Foreign Affairs*. He read them cover to cover and was up to date on political and business trends around the world. When my parents took their four-month, around-the-world cruises, as they did every year for twenty-five years, my father's secretary would send him packages of newspaper and magazine clippings that she knew he would find interesting. Every time the cruise ship reached a new destination, my parents would disembark and head straight for the post office, where Rivian's package of articles would be waiting.

Victor used every spare moment to keep himself informed and to satisfy his endless curiosity. On planes, he would bring stacks of magazines and newspapers to read. He also corresponded with businessmen, politicians, philanthropists, and other key figures around the world, thus adding to his prodigious information base. Part of his success was that he simply knew more about more things than most people. He foresaw trends because he availed himself of every piece of information available.

He also had a very strong constitution and always maintained excellent health. He was built like a Russian peasant—short in stature, with thick muscular legs, muscular arms and a strong and healthy heart. He had a large head—it was always hard to buy hats for him because his head was so big. I used to joke that he needed such a big head because he had such a big brain, and that may well have been true. His health and mindset were supported by the fact that he was never a worrier. He could sleep eight hours a night, untroubled by worries of any kind. He had a great attitude about life. When I was a child he would knock on my door and tell me that it was 7:00 a.m., time to start a new day—and he always spoke those words in a tone of excitement and freshness about the day ahead.

He was an intensely positive person. He was also physically fearless. He was never intimidated by the idea of germs—he didn't even believe in the whole concept of germs spreading disease. If I had a cold or anything else, my father would walk into my bedroom and put his arms around me. If any of his loved ones were sick, even with pneumonia, he would kiss that person right on the lips. His spirit was so large that nothing fazed him.

He also came from healthy stock. His father, Mark, was eighty-nine when he passed away, and longevity has always been a Kartozhinsky trait. My father used his enormous energy and his positive attitude about life to great advantage—he simply worked harder and smarter than anyone he came up against.

His honesty and straightforwardness, along with his abundant capacity for leadership, made him the de facto leader of our entire extended family. The Carter clan has a volatile, colorful side that evidenced itself on occasion. When there was a dispute that needed resolution, all sides routinely turned to my father to play the role of "honest broker."

One such story deserves mention. My father sought to resolve a long-standing business dispute related to Oscar Rudnick's business and finances. Over a period of seventeen years, Victor traveled repeatedly to Bakersfield to work to settle the disagreement. He did so not because he had a stake in the outcome or any sort of financial reward awaiting him if he were to succeed. Indeed, he received no compensation at all for those trips and all that effort—not even compensation for his travel expenses. He took on the responsibility of brokering a solution to a very complex problem simply as a tribute to the memory of the man who had helped his family get their business established in California back in the early 1920s. Seventeen years to resolve one (admittedly large) family business issue demonstrates another important aspect of my father's approach to life: When he committed to something, he was in all the way.

He always sought out people who would feed his mind, people who were like him, thinkers, interested in the world. A lifetime learner, he was also a great organizer of information, ideas, and people. The funny thing is that to the untrained eye, he might not have appeared the most organized of men. At the end of each working day, he would remove from his pockets many little pieces of paper on which he had scrawled practically illegible notes to himself. It was always left to someone else—a secretary or an assistant—to take those fragments and organize them into some sort of meaningful order. He might not have appeared on top of things to anyone who saw that system—but to underestimate him was never a wise move!

In fact, my father was incredibly organized, especially when it came to managing his time. He used every snippet of time to its maximum advantage. He was outstanding at delegating and chose competent people to have around him. When he made a handoff, he knew that the matter would be handled appropriately and quickly, without his needing to check up on things. He never micro-managed, and he ran meetings crisply, firmly, and decisively, without allowing others to speechify (often to their frustration, because many people do like to hear themselves talk in meetings).

His love of learning never ceased. In his later years, my husband, Jack, and I would go on cruises with my father. Jack is an outstanding sailor and won competitions for many years. As our cruise ship would enter a new part of the world, Jack and Victor would pore over the nautical charts and Jack would explain to my father intriguing aspects of the currents, the ocean depths, or other matters. It was all new to my father, and he was fascinated to learn new things.

Victor Carter possessed a perfect mix of hardheaded business thinking and truly extraordinary compassion for those who had less. To depict both sides of his nature, the philanthropic and the business-minded, I want to share the story of a worker I will call Enrique. This individual was one of Victor's "right-hand men" and a highly trusted employee at Carter Hardware, Vimcar, and for a short while at Builders Emporium. Years after Victor had sold his interest in Builders Emporium, Enrique called him at his office. Victor took the call without any delay, which amazed Enrique, because my father was such an important man. Enrique recounted to Hugh Sommers, my father's attorney, his surprise that Victor remembered everything about him, even though seventeen years had passed since Enrique left Victor's employ.

Since then, Enrique had had to have a leg amputated, and he contacted my father because he was scheduled for a second such operation the next day. He was deeply worried that if he died, creditors could take the family home, which he and his wife owned as a tenancy-in-common. He could think of no one else to call but my father.

The fact that someone in this position would think to call my father and would expect guidance or assistance from him illustrates the way my father was perceived by those whom he employed. He and Enrique spoke at eleven a.m., and my father immediately called Sommers. He told Sommers to create a trust, deeds, and other documents, so that if Enrique did in fact die as a result of this second operation, his widow would not have to fear losing her home. When Sommers asked how long he had to prepare all these documents, my father said, "I told Enrique that you'd be at the hospital to see him at two o'clock today."

Sommers dropped everything, because when my father told you to do something, it was never a mere suggestion. He met the two o'clock deadline, and Enrique signed off on the paperwork, thus allowing Sommers to record the deed that same day. Sad to say, Enrique did in fact die on the operating table, but his widow was able to keep her house.

The story doesn't end there. When my father received word that Enrique had died, he had Sommers visit Enrique's widow, explain the legal situation to her, and tell her that he, my father, would be in touch with her. He also instructed Sommers to see her every three months and provide a brief written report about how she was doing. All this for an employee he had not seen in seventeen years.

Two years later, Enrique's son called, wanting to borrow $900 to pay for tuition and books at UCLA. My father instructed Sommers to draw up loan documents for the requested amount. The terms were as follows: ten percent interest, payments on the interest only, with the balance due in three years. The young man came to Victor's office, agreed to the terms, signed the note, and received the money.

Naturally my father could have written a check for $900, especially as devoted as he was to the young man's family. That was not his way, however. He saw this as a teaching opportunity, to help a young person develop respect for the value of a dollar. In so doing, he was able to help a young man get a better start on his adult life.

My father was deeply interested in the way the human mind works. The field of psychology became part of the fabric of American culture in the 1940s and 1950s. My father was way ahead of the curve—as usual—employing psychologists to test and report back to him about his employees. He read voraciously on the subject of psychology, and we often discussed the topic. His interest in psychology may well have led me toward my career as a therapist. He was particularly curious about the practical applications of psychology. Theory and theoreticians interested him little. He did not admire those who taught theoretical fields like economics, especially if they had never gone out into the world and made money or met a payroll themselves. He had much more respect for people who were doers—builders, creators, scientists, engineers, those who had lofty purposes in life and worked hard to turn those dreams into reality. He did not respect those who had an education but did little with it to benefit society. He surrounded himself with people who thought big thoughts and accomplished big achievements. My father never thought small, and he had little interest in those who did.

At the same time, he had enormous will power. At one time in his life, he smoked three packs of cigarettes a day. His doctor told him that he risked losing a leg to circulatory problems if he didn't stop smoking. He never smoked another cigarette. He had a little toy cigarette that he would chew on, and you could tell when his mind was hard at work because of the crunching he gave that plastic cigarette.

Despite his love of learning, he was not always the greatest of conversationalists. He was always happy to give whatever information was asked of him, but he was not what one would term skilled in the art of repartee. I attribute this to the fact that English was not his first language and that he probably never achieved the level of comfort with the English language that he had with his native Russian.

. .
.

AS WE HAVE SEEN, his Russian heritage was the other major influence on my father's nature. He had a great Russian soul, loved Russian music and culture, and had a Russian sense of humor. He was not a joke teller. Rather, he found humor in the simple foibles of human beings, the scrapes that people got themselves into by force of their own personalities. He would laugh whenever he ran up against the kind of person defined in Yiddish as a *mazik*—a troublemaker, something of a difficult person. "Oh, you know Yankel," he would say with a grin. "He'll always try to do you one better. He'll always try to get one up on you." Or, "Oh, you know so-and-so. He's the one who's always trying to sell you ice in the wintertime."

His sense of humor was based on his forgiving nature. He never took it too seriously when someone tried to put one over on him. No one could succeed at that. Instead, he would simply smile at other people's weaknesses or frailties, accept these folks for who they were, and never take offense at behavior that was a natural outgrowth of the character of these individuals.

One time, a dentist told him that the fee for some work the dentist had performed would be $5,000, a figure that struck my father as exorbitant. When he asked the dentist to justify the fee, the dentist replied, "Oh, you can afford it." That was the wrong answer! Victor did not like being taken advantage of, and that was the last that that dentist saw of him. Conversely, my father became devoted at an early age to a particular tailor, Charles Tartaglia, who later was one of the leading tailors in Los Angeles. He patronized Tartaglia for decades, even when the tailor's eyesight had diminished so greatly that he could barely perform his work. If my father trusted you, you stayed on his good side for life.

Another revealing story involved the death of a close friend we'll call Eddie. Eddie was unmarried and had many "lady friends" (code for prostitutes) whom he saw with some frequency. After Eddie passed away, my father saw to it that the telephone company redirected to my father's private line all of the calls that came to his late friend's home, to ensure that if one of Eddie's "lady friends" called to ask why he had not been in contact lately, my father would be the one to speak with her. He wanted to protect the dignity of Eddie's memory. This unusual incident demonstrates my father's acceptance of others on their own terms.

Unlike most people, my father never saw problems as negatives. He saw them as opportunities to create new possibilities for himself, for us, and for his business ventures. He frequently told me, "Problems aren't bad things. They're just things that have to be solved. And I can solve as many as you want—but always just one problem at a time!"

17

My Parents' Marriage

TAKE THE GRACEFULNESS of Ginger Rogers and Fred Astaire, mix in the abiding affection of Spencer Tracy and Katharine Hepburn, and you have a good grasp on the nature of my parents' marriage. They were together for seventy-five years, longer than the life spans of many individuals. They had a beautiful marriage, a true love match, as strong and vibrant when they were in their nineties as when they eloped to Tijuana in their late teens. The marriage functioned as a well-designed system in which each partner played a clear part. My father handled the business and finance side, and my mother took care of everything else—the home, their clothes, their social calendar, and, above all, him!

My father was no more likely to comment on my mother's choices in terms of china, flowers, or dinner reservations than she was likely to opine about his latest business decision. Their marriage began at a time in our culture when gender roles were clearly defined, and they never veered from the comfort of the clear-cut roles they inhabited within their marriage. I would describe them as completely complementary to each other, a perfectly matched pair.

My mother was always proud of my father's accomplishments, and she guarded his time carefully. My father reciprocated her commitment with word, thought, and gesture. He made sure that she had the best of everything—the finest clothes, the most attractive home, and luxurious travel arrangements. He enjoyed shopping with her, sitting in the "husband's chair" in the most exclusive stores, looking approvingly as Adrea modeled one beautiful outfit after another. One time, early in their marriage, my mother bought some clothes on sale. My father was deeply disturbed. He told her, "Never buy clothes on sale! If you find what you like, pay full price, and buy it in every color!"

Today the term "trophy wife" has come into vogue. It implies that a highly successful businessman has taken an attractive wife considerably his junior, that she is the "trophy" for all of his efforts in the business world. In my parents' marriage, my father considered my mother his trophy more than half a century after they met. He adored her, lavished her with every conceivable gift, and never wanted to be apart from her.

· ·

AT THE SAME TIME, my mother considered her primary responsibility in life to be taking care of my father. She would select and lay out his clothes. He cared little about how he looked. She was the keeper of the wardrobe and his fashion consultant, overseeing matters when he changed sizes in clothes. She was always trying to make over his appearance, but with little success, because he was born without a shred of vanity. He was always an attractive man, always appropriately dressed—thanks to her!—but clothing did not interest him.

My mother played with consummate ease the role of the gracious wife, vivacious hostess, and adventurous travel partner. She had come from modest circumstances. Her parents certainly did not have the financial wherewithal that my mother enjoyed in her marriage. She was delighted to travel first-class all over the world with my father, to shop at the finest stores, to entertain on a regal scale, to welcome luminaries into her home, and simply to have a great time with her husband and their friends. My parents had such a strong marriage that all the men they knew wanted to be Victor and all the women wanted to be Adrea. Often, the reality of a marriage is very different from its outward appearance. Yet in my parents' case, their marriage truly was as spectacular as it appeared.

They were savvy people, always a step ahead of the crowd. In contemporary terms, they would be called "early adapters"— open to new ideas and new ways of doing things. They were the first to own a co-op apartment in a high-rise building on Wilshire Boulevard. (They bought the unit, Penthouse A, sight unseen from the builders, the Tishman brothers, who described it to them over the phone while they were on a cruise.) They were among the first to own a convertible and a television set and take round-the-world cruises, and later they were the first to fly the Concorde. My father had a phone in his car and installed a swimming pool in his backyard decades before anyone else. As soon as mink coats came on the market, my father bought the nicest possible one for my mother.

Their civic involvements brought them enormous pleasure and satisfaction, whether it was my father starting Brentwood Country Club with a few of his friends, or my mother's role as the president of the Music Commission for the City of Los Angeles. They served either on the board or in some other important capacity with the Los Angeles Philharmonic for more than sixty years.

My parents intensely disliked being apart. This was difficult during the early years of their marriage, when my father's business responsibilities kept him out in the evenings. My mother would accompany him on his business trips whenever she could. In addition to traveling with him, she also brought music into the home and joy into his life. She had an extraordinary appetite for culture and the arts and went with him to the theater, the ballet, and orchestral concerts. Much to my delight, I often joined my mother at performances when my father was unavailable because of his work commitments. My mother's mother was a piano teacher and instilled in her a love of fine music, which she passed along to me. She and I would harmonize as we sang my father's native Russian songs, and this delighted him.

My parents had little interest in traditional religious matters. The two of them were devoted to Judaism, but they were secular Jews. Her family was not especially religious, and my father's family, after leaving Russia, had little regular contact with traditional forms of Judaism.

They were proud Jews, and deeply spiritual people, but religion was not how they expressed the wellsprings of spirituality within them. They were not the type to have deep philosophical discussions or debates about the issues of the day. You could say their marriage "rode the waves"—they knew how to keep things light. This was an important gift, considering that the first two decades of their marriage were overshadowed by the illness and then the loss of their son.

Because my parents had eloped, it had always been a dream of my mother's to have a formal wedding. At their fiftieth anniversary, they finally had the ceremony—very different from when they had awakened a justice of the peace in Tijuana to pronounce them man and wife.

My father, sixty-eight years old, and my mother, sixty-seven, along with three hundred of their closest friends, relatives, and business associates, took over the Hillcrest County Club and had an elaborate wedding ceremony. My mother decided that I would be the maid of honor and their three granddaughters would serve as flower girls. Remarkably, her father, Morris, who would live to be 101, was present at this fiftieth anniversary party, an experience to which few men can lay claim.

My parents' wedding included everything you would find at any Jewish wedding—the rabbi pronounced the vows, my father stepped on the glass, and the experience was highly emotional and moving. That night, my mother realized a long-held dream. I'm sure it did not matter as much to my father to go through with the wedding ceremony. His primary interest in the event was simply to make her happy, and that he did.

. .

I STARTED THIS CHAPTER by mentioning Tracy and Hepburn. When my parents were talking with each other or kidding around, you could see similarities between their relationship and those of the two stars of the silver screen. My mother would call my father either Vic (a name that practically no one else on earth dared to use) or she would call him by his last name. "Carter," she would say, "what do you think of that?"

It was always entertaining for me when my mother called my father by his last name. In turn, my father called my mother "A." Once he got home, he liked to sit in one chair and not get up. So when I heard my father calling, "A!" it meant that he wanted my mother to bring him some tea, a meal, or something else. He was a pasha in the home, and my mother loved playing the role of the pasha's lover. She told me not long ago, "I kept a man happy for a lifetime, and for a woman, that's a successful life." This is obviously not a sentiment that would be seconded by the feminist movement, but it certainly worked in their marriage, and for the times into which they had been born.

My parents were extremely proud of their three grandchildren, all of whom have advanced degrees. Sheri Silverton has a master's degree in library science and a son, Devin Jackson; Leigh Silverton has a doctorate in psychology; and Robin Buckner has a law degree and two children, Katherine and William. My parents always enjoyed Sunday evening buffets, Thanksgiving dinners, and the occasional Passover meal with their children and grandchildren at the Hillcrest Country Club. My father gave his grandchildren the *World Book Encyclopedia*, to encourage them to become knowledgeable about the world around them, and stressed his commitment to the strength and survival of the State of Israel. He shared with them his optimistic nature and his lifetime love of reading and learning. He would tell them to "think a smile," and he would place his hand on their foreheads, intoning in a dramatic voice the words, "Grow! Contribute! Earn!" Today, his grandchildren contribute to the world in important ways.

. .

MY FATHER WAS AN ENTHUSIASTIC grandfather to my children, especially after my marriage to their father ended. One of their favorite early childhood memories is of Santa appearing each Christmas, with bags of candy and toys for them. It took them a while to realize that Santa, walking hand in hand with their mother, was their grandfather in disguise!

As I write these words, my mother is ninety-five. Although her mental faculties are not precisely what they once were, she is as graceful and elegant as ever. Her skin is free of wrinkles and her eyes shine with the same beauty that she possessed as the teenage girl who stole my father's heart. Even today, midway through her tenth decade, she is always appropriate in every social situation. It must be extremely difficult for her not to have my father alongside her—how do you cope with the loss of a partner of seventy-five years?

My parents had beautiful parties to celebrate their seventieth and seventy-fifth wedding anniversaries. At the celebration for their seventy-fifth anniversary, they could no longer wander the floor together, holding hands, moving from table to table to greet their friends and associates. My father was ninety-three and my mother ninety-two, and their guests came to them. When my father first spied my mother, sewn into that red velvet pillowslip, back when they and their world were young, an eternal love story ignited, and for all those who knew my parents, the glory of that love will always illuminate the world.

18

Being Victor Carter's Daughter

As I grew up, my experiences with my father were transcendent, and we shared a rare bond. My father had a much easier time relating to women than to men, because of the closeness of his relationship with his mother. When she passed away shortly after his marriage, the loss left a gap in his life that I was destined to fill. He even named me after her. It became clear to me—not then, but later on—that we would enjoy the same connection of spirit that he shared with her.

Temperamentally, my father and I are a lot alike. We also look alike: My lips are like his, my smile is his. And our thinking patterns are similar. I resemble my mother in many important ways and I cherish the bond we shared. Yet my attachment to my father was so strong that my mother sometimes looked at us in amusement and said, "Like father, like daughter."

He and I found it fascinating to dissect what people did, why they did it, and what it all meant. The actions and motivations of others were endlessly fascinating to the two of us. My mother would sometimes roll her eyes at our endless psychologizing.

The unique connection between my father and me existed from the start. When I was born, my father burst into the delivery room—at the time, an unheard-of place for a husband—and held me. His first words to me, he would often tell me later, were "You're just what I wanted." He had lost his mother, and he wanted a girl, and I was fortunate enough to be that girl.

We were extremely close throughout my childhood. I remember that when I was a small child I had a fear of taking baths. My father, who was, needless to say, an extremely busy man, took a whole day off from work and got in the bathtub with me, with the intent of teaching me not just to take baths but to *enjoy* them. It took him the better part of a day, just the two of us in the bathroom, but eventually his persistence paid off. I took my bath! My mother says she had never seen anyone's fingers so wrinkled as my father's were after all those hours in the tub.

I have already mentioned that at age eight I would cook breakfast for my father as he told of his experiences in Rostov-on-Don. It was clear to me even then that, aside from my mother, I was the only person to whom he could safely tell those stories. It gave me a sense of importance and value because my father trusted me with these painful memories. A few years later, when I reached adolescence, we had a very different kind of conversation. I must have been about twelve years old and I was totally innocent of any knowledge of sex. The boy next door had chosen to fill in that gap in my knowledge and did so with expressions that were accurate and to the point, but nonetheless somewhat gross and frightening! He used a four-letter word to describe lovemaking, and both the word and what it stood for were certainly eye-opening for me. I decided that the four-letter word he had shared with me was a bad word, and that meant that the whole business was bad. I went to my parents to ask them about this, and my mother sensed that my father might be the best person with whom to discuss the issue.

He turned out to be the perfect person.

My father sat me down and told me what sex was all about—in general terms, to be sure. The striking thing was that he was not the least bit embarrassed about discussing sex with me. I remember him telling me, "It's beautiful! It's really a wonderful thing. It's the closest two people can get. It's a way of showing love."

What a sensitive way to handle a delicate topic with a twelve-year-old. I was fine with the issue after that.

Not long after my father explained the facts of life to me, I met my first boyfriend, Joe. He was a minister's son, and all the clichés about the "preacher's son" were true about this young man. He was a wild guy, even at age twelve. He gave me my first kiss. We played spin the bottle on Halloween, and the bottle somehow always pointed at me!

He came over to our house one time and broke a window. My father called him in, sat him down at the dinner table, and asked how he planned to pay for the damage. Well, this was the last thing Joe expected. I guess he had been getting off the hook for everything he had done all his life, but he had never come up against the likes of my father. Joe had no idea how to respond.

My father told him, "I won't tell your dad, if you take care of this yourself. So how are you going to pay for this?"

You can imagine this poor twelve-year-old boy, just squirming in his seat at our dinner table! Nevertheless, they made an agreement under which Joe would pay my father twenty-five cents a week. My father held him to that deal, too. He did so because he thought that this young man needed to learn to take responsibility for his actions. He was just a naughty little kid, a minister's son who liked doing outrageous things. And don't you know that, since Joe had a little bit of "bad boy" in him, I really liked him!

At first I was embarrassed that my father was taking the whole thing so seriously. After a while, though, it dawned on me that it was courageous—and highly original—of him to handle the situation that way. Most parents would go right to the other parent, who would discipline the child. Joe definitely didn't want my father to deal directly with his father. He probably would have gotten a thrashing. So my father found this wonderfully wise way of working the whole thing out.

Throughout my teenage years, my father and I grew even closer. We began to travel more as a family after Bobby passed away, first to places like Palm Springs, which, back in the 1940s, had pretty much only one hotel for out-of-town visitors. The world certainly has changed! Later, we would travel to Hawaii, and in still later years, I joined my father and mother on some of their cruises.

It was always an adventure to dine or to travel with my parents, either as a teenager or an adult. My father took enormous pleasure in entering into the customs of the groups he met when he traveled the world. One time, my parents took Jack and me along on a trip to New Zealand. While Jack was off sailing, my parents and I went to visit a Maori village where we discovered, to the great discomfort of my mother and myself, that visitors were expected to rub noses with every member of the tribe.

My mother and I hesitated, of course, but my father jumped right in with great gusto, gleefully rubbing noses with all present. This gave me the courage to follow suit, and even my elegant mother rubbed noses, an experience she surely could have lived without.

．．
．

AFTER LUNCH, THE MEN OF THE VILLAGE presented us a show of their warrior abilities and techniques. My father jumped right up on stage and stomped around in mock warrior fashion, to the delight of all present. He always wanted to taste the local foods—porcini mushrooms in September in Italy, roasted pig in Hawaii, baklava in the Middle East. He was more than a tourist—he was a true adventurer. My mother and I shared his love of new vistas and new experiences.

My father had a wonderful way with all women, myself included. He always made me feel beautiful, and he did the same for every woman he met. He had loved his mother and from that relationship he developed the capacity to give women the benefit of the doubt in every situation, to find ways to accept them as they were, without looking for shortcomings or criticizing. Of course, if he thought a woman wasn't fair to men, my father did not like that, either.

He always gave me the feeling that I was going to grow up to be something special. I remember being president of a club in high school, at a time when my father was traveling in Japan. He sent me a long telegram congratulating me because we had raised money for the City of Hope. He was doubly proud because, at the time, the City of Hope was his most important charitable endeavor. I still have that telegram. I will be forever grateful to him for the sense he gave me that I matter as a person, because I mattered so much to him.

Our friendship had its competitive side as well, which evidenced itself in the games we played. As a boy, my father rode wild horses in Russia, and as a teenager and in his early twenties, he carried those hundred-pound kegs of nails around Carter Hardware. After those kegs, he was not enamored of physical exercise—with a few exceptions. One was Ping-Pong. He and I were fierce Ping-Pong warriors, and we would play game after game in the backyard, often going to tie-breakers, because our skills were so evenly matched. My father had the ability, when serving, to make a Ping-Pong ball spin in ways that I've never seen elsewhere. As a family, we also loved to play gin rummy and sometimes bridge. We competed hard against each other, and that was a part of our friendship, too.

As I got into my later teenage years, my father had become so successful in business and so important in the Jewish community that people constantly wanted favors from him. These favor-seekers included friends of mine and people who might have wanted to be my friend simply to get closer to my father. It was often embarrassing for me when people asked me for favors from him, because I never knew what to tell them. How was I to know if my father wanted to grant a particular favor or had interest in a particular business endeavor? My father, realizing my discomfort, told me, "Don't worry about it at all. You just send them to me. If I want to say no, I'll say no. It's fine." Thus I was able to overcome that sense of responsibility I had because I was, in fact, Victor Carter's daughter.

Children of famous and successful parents have huge advantages in life—a financially comfortable childhood, connections, a path in life that has been made smooth because of the success of their mother or father. Yet there is also a challenge to having a famous and successful parent. People have higher expectations of those children than children from more "normal" families. When I was traveling with my father, it was always a badge of honor for me when people said, admiringly, "Oh, you're Victor Carter's daughter!" As I came into my own adulthood, though, it became something of a burden. Suddenly people were looking at me, as they look at the offspring of all successful people, saying, "Well, so what are *you* all about?" and "So what have *you* done lately?"

. .

MUCH IS EXPECTED in a public way. You must not shame your parents, you must add to their luster, and you must not detract from their reputation. The constellation of expectations arising for the children of famous or successful parents takes you further away from yourself as an individual, from your true identity.

It took me some time to realize that my own identity would be formed by *who I was as a person*, not by standing in the reflected glory of my remarkable father. In many ways, the first part of my adult life was a journey toward finding out who the authentic "me" was. Ironically, when I began to discover my authentic self—by getting my degrees in psychology, developing a successful practice, and finding my true love, Jack—I enjoyed even more of my father's approval than I ever had. I went from a person who shaped her nature to please her father to someone who had discovered her real nature. Ironically, in so doing, I pleased my father even more.

Several stories from this period illustrate the point. After I had completed my master's degree in psychology at Pepperdine University, I decided to persue a doctorate, and my father agreed to pay for this phase of my education. I enrolled in a program that turned out to be something less than ideal and I told my father that I intended to transfer to another school. To my surprise and disappointment, he said that if I changed programs, he would not pay for the new program.

Similarly, when my divorce ended the lease on a rather expensive Jaguar that I had been driving, my father bought me a garden variety Ford. That Ford had a license plate with the letters FUB, and I always thought of that car as "the FUB," unimpressive and average after my beautiful Jag. Finally, after my grandfather Mark died, I wanted to buy a house with my bequest. I needed financial help from my father to swing a deal on an attractive home, but he refused.

The thread that connects these three stories is that my father wanted me to live in reality and to succeed on my own. I completed a Ph.D., which I paid for out of my own income. I eventually bought a beautiful BMW to replace the FUB. And Jack and I bought a "fixer-upper" on a less-than-desirable block, which we improved so beautifully that my father was moved to contribute a new roof and a pool. When it came to paying for my education, my car, and my house, my father wanted me to experience the taste of success on my own terms and not with his help. This was one of the greatest gifts he ever gave me: the pleasure and pride of succeeding on my own initiative. I will always thank him for this.

When vanity license plates became available, my parents ordered them with their initials on them. My mother's plates read

AZC, and my father's plates were VMC-33. I never thought much about the "33" part of the plate until Jack came along. He instantly understood the meaning of that number: It was the year of my birth. My father wanted to include me even in that unique way. My father confirmed Jack's theory, and when my father stopped driving, Jack assumed the license plates that read VMC-33.

And now my father is gone. Or at least he's not with us in the same way as before. After my brother passed away, I stopped making a distinction between *here* and *there*. I used to think that *there* was way up there somewhere, and now I realize it's really all around us. There isn't that much of a difference between this plane and the other plane. I have always been very close to my dad on an emotional level, and that holds true now that he is with us in a different way.

Were he to think about this book, I'm sure he would wonder why his life was important enough for anyone else to read about it. That's just the way he always saw himself, his inherent modesty shining through. At the same time, I know that he would want me to have a good time, both with the writing of this book and with the business of living life. He was always adamant that we were meant to enjoy our existences. So I know he's still here around us, laughing and saying, "Take life seriously—but not too seriously. Why should I have had all the fun? Now it's your turn."

Of all the gifts my father gave me, the greatest gift was this understanding of life. Yes, life is serious and full of responsibilities, and we have an obligation to contribute to the betterment of the world around us. At the same time, though, life is to be enjoyed. We're here to have fun. And he did.

19

Final Years

IN THE 1910S, AS A BOY, my father learned the hardware business in his native Rostov-on-Don.

In the 1920s, not yet a teenager, he helped as his family fled Russia for Los Angeles, and he worked with his father to establish Carter Hardware in downtown L.A.

In the 1930s, as a husband and father, he went off on his own and created Vimcar, his first successful business venture.

In the 1940s, as a businessman, he turned Vimcar into a major wartime supplier to the U.S. government and then turned Builders Emporium into the nation's first hardware superstore. He also shared his technical knowledge, business contacts, and growing fortune with a nascent State of Israel.

In the 1950s, as a national business leader, he turned a failing film studio into the Republic Corporation, one of the most successful companies traded on the New York Stock Exchange.

In the 1960s, as a humanitarian, he played a major role in the civil rights era as a friend and supporter of the Rev. Martin Luther King Jr. and Medgar Evers, and he played a major role in providing Israel with financial, moral, and business support before, during, and after the Six Day War.

In the 1970s and 1980s, he continued to serve the business world as a director on the boards of major corporations and continued to serve the Jewish and secular philanthropic communities of Los Angeles as a leader, organizer, major donor, and inspirational role model for men of his generation and for those who followed.

In the 1990s, my father remained active and vigorous, physically and intellectually.

In the first decade of the 21st century, he still possessed the energy to travel to Israel to dedicate the Tel Aviv University Youth Orchestra, for which he was the principal donor. Even in his nineties, he was still going strong.

A life for the ages.

. .

INTO HIS EIGHTIES, he and my mother traveled the world, either on their cruises or on their visits to Israel, which they still made twice or three times a year. He used a carry-on Louis Vuitton tote bag perfect for his news magazines, business periodicals, and anything else that fed his never-ending quest for knowledge. I treasure that bag today, because it was always with him. By his eighties, however, my father began to slow down, which only makes sense, given how deeply involved he had been for so many decades with family, business, philanthropy, culture, and his friends. I see this as a normal, healthy psychological process that happens to us all. It's nature's way of saying, "Come on, now, you don't have to expend all this energy. It's time instead to receive the reward for all you have given throughout your life. Why not conserve your energy for those people and things that matter the most to you?"

Even highly productive people like my father, toward the end of their lives, find ways of conserving energy. By the time he reached his early nineties, his process of detaching from the worlds of business and philanthropy, and from most activities that were not directly related to family life, was essentially complete. His office continued to make donations to countless organizations, but his day-to-day involvement and leadership roles with charitable and philanthropic organizations had ceased.

Even at the end of their lives, my parents remained extraordinarily close and devoted. When they were both in wheelchairs, they would still hold hands. If they were at a distance, they would throw kisses to each other from across the room. When my father's health required the installation of a hospital bed in their bedroom, he insisted that it be placed directly next to my mother's bed, so that they could hold hands there, too. Their affection was undiminished by time. My mother was able to continue her yoga practice with private classes at home, even into her nineties. I can still see my father waiting just outside the living room for her to finish her yoga class, so that he could be with her once more.

Shortly after the love story that was my parents' marriage reached its seventy-fifth year, my father encountered his final illness. My mother, my husband, Jack, and I were together with my father when he passed away in the hospital. I held his hand the entire time, and I was whispering in his ear, "You did so well, you had such a great life, Dad. You helped so many people. You can be proud of what you did. And everybody loves you."

I continued to talk to him for about an hour and a half. I don't know if he could hear or understand anything, because he was in the state that preceded his passing. I want to believe that he did hear me as I shared my love with him directly, in this manner, for the last time. Yet I believe the connection I made with him in our last conversation was more than a physical speaking and hearing of words. As I spoke with him for the last time, I felt our souls commingling on a level of vibration, and I sensed his ability to hear me on a metaphysical level far removed from the limited realm of the senses. I had a sense of recognition from him, beyond words and normal consciousness, one last time in this earth plane, and I know that the bond we felt was powerful and eternal. As he had told me, at my birth, that I was just what he wanted, I told him, in that final exchange of love, that *he* was just what *I* had wanted.

I will also always remember the last words that Jack said to my dad: "Good night, my big brother." We were with him to the end. One moment, we were listening to his breathing, and then just like that he was gone.

He passed away at 7:23 p.m. on March 27, 2004. The Hebrew word for passing is *niftar*, which is derived from the term meaning "to be free of one's obligations in life." No one had discharged life's obligations with greater success, dignity, and élan than my father.

Some people come into the world and leave it a better place. From the customers at Carter Hardware who needed some nails for a project in their backyard to the board of directors of Teva, from Vimcar to Builders Emporium to the Republic Corporation, and even going all the way back to the search for mineral water for his mother on the streets of Constantinople, my father made this world a decidedly better place.

I hope this story inspires you to ask, "What can *I* do to improve the lives of those around me? How can *I* help the members of my family? How can *I* serve my community and the world?"

The breadth of my father's vision inspires us all to increase the scope of our own vision, to see where we can make things better for those we love and for those we have never met. That was my father's mission, and from my vantage point, all I can think to say is this: "Dad, mission accomplished."

I want to share with you two memorials to my father. The first is a front-page article from the *Wave*, an African-American newspaper based in Los Angeles. It appeared on March 31, 2004, shortly after my father's passing. The second is the eulogy spoken by Rabbi Jacob Pressman, who presided at my father's funeral on that same day.

SERVICES HELD FOR VICTOR M. CARTER

By Betty Pleasant
WAVE COMMUNITY NEWSPAPERS

LOS ANGELES – Funeral services were held Wednesday for Victor M. Carter, the white man who had [a greater] impact on the black community of Los Angeles than any of the African Americans in it. Carter, a highly honored humanitarian, was a giant in the black community, beginning in the early 1960s, through his leadership roles in the Urban League and the NAACP, and continuing thereafter with his shaping of black politicians and political policies that empowered the city's African Americans.

"Victor Carter was one of those visionary people who was not frightened by the demographic changes that were facing this city," said former Councilman Robert Farrell, who worked with Carter on many issues. "In fact, he was part of the responsible leadership that gave time and energy to the development of the black communities."

Carter engineered the political rise of Tom Bradley and was Bradley's closest advisor and confidant throughout Bradley's terms on the City Council and his 20 years as mayor. Carter was a respected advisor and co-organizer—with the legendary Marnesba Tackett—of the campaigns to desegregate the Los Angeles Unified School District and to end housing discrimination in the Crenshaw District and in outlying areas such as Compton and Inglewood.

A consummate volunteer, Carter was tapped for civic duty as a harbor commissioner and as a member of the board of directors of the Southern California Rapid Transit District (now the MTA). He was president of the Fire Commission and is credited with having rooted out institutional racism in the Fire Department. The Los Angeles Fire Department was integrated under his stewardship and equal treatment of all its employees became an established policy.

Early in the 1960s, Carter was called upon to serve on a special committee convened to seek ways of improving the then-volatile relations between law enforcement and the black community. He figured the raging hostility between the two sides would be eased if a black man became a police commissioner.

Carter, then, became instrumental in the appointment of Henri O'Bryant as the first African American on the Police Commission.

Carter was a forceful advocate of civil rights who organized local blacks and whites to join the Rev. Martin Luther King's movement to desegregate the South. He spearheaded the establishment of a scholarship fund for the children of Medgar Evers, the Mississippi NAACP president who was murdered for his civil rights activities, and, when the pre-arranged financing for the trip suddenly fell through, Carter raised the money to send 12 busloads of Angelenos to the historic March on Washington in 1963.

"There are a lot of examples of how he supported what he believed in ... with his funds, as well as with his leadership and his advice to people who were working to make this a better community," Farrell noted.

"He spent a lot of money in our community," commented journalist Libby Clark, who covered L.A. blacks' early quest for power. "Victor Carter was in the middle of every dog fight we had."

In addition to his leadership role in the black community's civil rights and political struggles, Carter had a significant role in advancing the community's aspirations for economic opportunities. Toward that end, he focused on providing educational and job training opportunities to young people who had been victims of past discrimination.

He helped create Operation Bootstrap on Central Avenue, to train young blacks for industrial jobs. He helped establish an office and community center for SLANT (Self Leadership for All Nations Today), to take black youths off the streets and away from gangs and into training and employment, and he co-chaired the Interracial Council for Business Opportunity, which paired local white businesses with minorities interested in establishing their own businesses.

"He was a great champion of human rights, civil rights and a decent human being," said Urban League President John Mack upon learning of Carter's death this week. "He truly cared about all people, no matter who they were. He was extremely generous financially, but he did more than write a check, he became personally involved and worked hard to build bridges of mutual respect and understanding."

"Victor was a leader for all seasons and one of a kind," Mack said. "He left a great legacy throughout the entire city of Los Angeles and certainly in our community. He was a leadership example that others need to emulate."

The Victor M. Carter Humanitarian Award was created by United Way Inc. in his honor several years ago, and is bestowed by the organization to "an individual who has both enhanced and embraced the community and who has been the most significant contributor to improving the quality of life through bettering the relationships of all people in the Greater Los Angeles community."

Services for Carter, who was the founder of Builders Emporium and owner of Republic Pictures, were held at Mount

Sinai Memorial Park. He is survived by his wife, Adrea;
daughter, Dr. Fanya Carter; three grandchildren, three great-
grandchildren and a brother (sic—actually, a sister).

· ·
·

RABBI PRESSMAN OFFERED SOME PERSONAL INSIGHTS as he
captured the essence of my father's life:

"IT IS A LONG WAY from Rostov-on-Don to this hilltop in
the westernmost part of the Western world, but hilltops
have been the natural habitat of Victor M. Carter. Whatever challenges faced him in his life or the world around
him, Victor invariably reached for the top and achieved it.
Whether it was from the penthouse of the Wilshire Ter-
race, or the penthouse of the Moriah Hotel in Jerusalem,
Victor could look around him 360 degrees and know that
he was responsible for enormous healing and growth and
development in the panorama before him. He instinctively
spent his life performing the classical Jewish mitzvah of
tikkun olam, repairing the broken places in the world. It is
patently impossible to narrate in our brief memorial here
the entire scope of the ways in which this man changed the
world as he found it. It would take, and should take, a very
thick volume to create a biography in his name.

"His roots go back to the successful life of his grandparents in business in Russia, which enabled them to live beyond the Pale of Settlement. There, he was born to Mark
and Fanya Carter, the middle child and only boy in a family
of four girls—Shura, Marie, Mathilde, and Bella, only one
of whom survives and is too frail to attend. The family left
Russia in the midst of the turbulence during and after the
Russian Revolution, and settled here. I still remember

what a stalwart of the burgeoning Jewish community here in Southern California was Mark.

"Victor began to work in the family business, leaving school in his teens to do so. It was apparently predestined, *bashert,* that there he should meet the daughter of one of his father's customers, a beautiful girl named Adrea. Characteristically, when Victor saw a good thing, he acted on it. Five days later, they were married. Would it last? It only lasted for seventy-five years, but they have given the community an example of a man and a woman living and working in harmony to the very last moment which has been the envy and the inspiration of their friends.

"Nothing is perfect. They suffered the loss of a son, Bobby, who died at the age of seventeen, a victim of muscular dystrophy. Their consolation has been their daughter, Fanya. When she was first placed in Victor's arms, he held her hand and said, "You are beautiful. You are just what I wanted. I love you already." Fanya, named for her grandmother, has been a great source of pride to Victor and Adrea, and invaluable in these recent years when their strength began to fail. Dr. Fanya's career in counseling others, her husband, Jack Delchamps, her children—Sheri, Leigh, and Robin; and her grandchildren, their great-grandchildren—Devin, William, and Katherine—brought new pleasures into their life.

. .

"To RETURN TO THE EARLIER YEARS, Victor eventually left Carter Hardware to venture on his own, first into a window sash business, then into the creation of the very first self-service super-hardware store ever: the Builders Emporium. As a former customer, I can attest that nothing since measured up to the friendly atmosphere of that store and its satellites. It was a giant step from that to his taking over the sagging fortunes of Republic Pictures and turning it into the Republic Corporation.

"Throughout the years, he reached across racial, religious, and national lines—Jewish, Christian, Black, Asian, or Hispanic—to make the human lot easier. To best convey the number and the variety of his causes, you have only to walk into a narrow hallway in their home, and see modestly displayed there the incredible number of plaques, government citations, and medals bestowed upon him.

"There are Gold Keys from the Jewish Community Council's campaigns, which he headed one way or another for years. He served as its president, was cited by the United Jewish Appeal. From Ben-Gurion and Golda Meir to every top Israel political leader, he was their cherished friend upon whom they leaned in year after year of crisis, war, and growth.

"His concern for the black community was singular. Examples: Victor, during his term as Los Angeles Fire Commissioner, removed racial discrimination from the Fire Department. An early member of the Urban League and the National Association for the Advancement of Colored People, he fought to improve relations between the black community and the police and sheriff's departments. He helped establish SLANT (Self Leadership for All Nationalities Today) and initiated the growth of Operation Bootstrap. I well remember his creating schools for training young people for better industrial jobs in Watts and South Central. When Medgar Evers was assassinated, he arranged scholarships for his children. When Rev. Martin Luther King Jr. began his fight for equality, Victor organized leaders here to support him. When the March on Washington, which produced the "I have a dream" challenge, was about to be canceled for lack of money for buses, Victor raised the money to finance it.

"He served for several years as president of the Japan-America Society, helped found the Japanese Philharmonic Orchestra in L.A. A beautiful medal from the emperor hangs in his hall for receiving 'The Third Order of the Imperial Treasure.' There also hang there a gold medal presented him by Prime Minister Levi Eshkol of Israel; the 'Sword of Israel' award; evidence of an honorary doctorate conferred upon him after four years as chairman of the board of governors of Tel Aviv University. His efforts on behalf of the Hispanic community were lauded by the city and state. Here at home, he chaired the United Way, and for all his humanitarian work, an annual award was established by the United Way in his name, the Victor M. Carter Humanitarian Award, and in 1988, they honored him with their Alexis de Tocqueville Award.

"These were not empty honors. He got them the hard way. He earned them.

"Both my wife and I can testify from personal experience what responsibility this man felt to *tikkun olam*. When before, during, and after the 1967 Six Day War in which the world waited silently for Israel to be destroyed by her neighbors roundabout, I was bemoaning with Victor the lack of good public relations we felt Israel always suffered. He immediately gave me a large amount of seed money to organize a pro-Israel propaganda machine for which Nathan Shapell provided offices. With it, we were able to create overnight an agency to inform radio and television newspersons of the truth, write scripts for talk show hosts to answer the hate calls they were receiving, write the text of telegrams to bombard our government to come to Israel's aid, and change public opinion which was running against us. We worked for three months, successfully, the product of a Jew who cared and dared innovate.

"Around the same time, he undertook the leadership of a great victory concert of the Israel Philharmonic to be held in a matter of a few short weeks at the Hollywood Bowl. When my wife, Margie, offered to help, he was grateful because he told her he had no troops to assist him in this gigantic effort. She worked with him in selling out the Bowl with Jascha Heifetz and Jack Benny as co-attractions with the Israel Philharmonic. She can attest to the 'hands on' managerial and philanthropic talents of this man.

"Having said all this, I have not begun to tell the story of Victor Carter, a giant among men. That vision of him made it all the more difficult to see him yielding to the wheelchair as age crept up on him. We who watched realized that we may never see such another man soon who embraced the world with his breadth of caring. A strong-minded, no-nonsense business tycoon, with a warm and loving heart for humanity, starting with family.

. .

"IT WAS APPROPRIATE, THEREFORE, that his declining days were blessed with the gathering around him of those who loved him. The last hours of his life were spent with Adrea holding one hand and Fanya holding the other, whispering in his ear, 'We are here. We love you. You have led a remarkable and worthwhile life. And now you are going peacefully into the light.' They held on to him until his very last breath and beyond. Interesting, when Fanya was born, he held her hand and whispered loving words into her tiny ear; and at life's end, she was holding his. I choose to believe that as the light of his life flickered, somehow he heard and he knew those he loved were escorting him like a Biblical king into the quiet unknown.

"Sadly, the blessing of a very long life also means that many who knew him have long since preceded him in death. Their souls overflow this chapel, and with them the tens of thousands of human beings whose lives were touched and made better because of him.

"Victor M. Carter: a man who incorporated so successfully into his life the best of the Jewish virtue of *tikkun olam,* repairing the broken world, and made the world better for his having lived. From the high place to which he has now gone may we hope that he will see us use his memory as an inspiration to carry on the good works which he performed in his long and very full lifetime. May his soul be bound up in the bond of eternal life."

Appendix

IN THE CHAPTER on my father's philanthropic endeavors, I mentioned the existence of two index card files, each a foot long, that listed his charitable donations to thousands of organizations and institutions over half a century. Just to get a sense of the breadth of his donations, I include here a small sample of that list of organizations. These constitute the first half inch of cards in the first of the two foot-long files—a small portion of the charitable institutions filed under the letter "A":

ACLU

Adat Ariel

Anti-Defamation League

Achievable Foundation

Agudath Israel of America

AIDS Healthcare Foundation

AIDS Project LA (every year)

AIDS Walk LA

Alcoholism Council of Greater Los Angeles

ALI Israel Society for Crippled Children

Alternate Living for the Aged

Alzheimer's Association

Alzheimer's Research

AMNA Women's Council

Amanda Foundation

America-Israel Cultural Foundation

American Academic Association

American Academy of the Arts in Europe

American Associates Ben-Gurion University

American Association for Ethiopian Jews

American Association for Middle Eastern Studies

American Association for the United Nations Pacific Chapter

American Cancer Society

American Committee for the Beersheva Foundation

American Committee for Modern Talmud Additions

American Committee for the Tel Aviv Foundation

American Committee for the Weizmann Institute of Science

American Diabetes Association

American Foundation for the Blind

American Foundation for Neurologic Disease

American Friends of Aish Hatorah

American Friends of the Alliance Israelite Universelle

American Friends of Bet Hatefutsoth (the Diaspora Museum in Tel Aviv)

American Friends of Boys Town Jerusalem

American Friends of Hebrew University

American Friends of the Israel
National Museum of Science

American Friends of the
Israel Museum

American Friends of the Israel
Philharmonic Orchestra

American Friends of the Jerusalem
College of Technology

American Friends of Rechov Sum
Sum, Sesame St., Inc.

American Friends of Shalva

American Friends of the Tel Aviv
Museum of Art

American Friends of the Tel Aviv
Museum and Other Museums

American Friends of Tel Aviv
University—Adrea & Victor
Carter Philharmonic

THE FOLLOWING IS A PARTIAL LIST of Victor M. Carter's key involvements supporting Israel:

Chairman Emeritus/Founder, American Friends of Tel Aviv University

Director, Ben Gurion University

Director, Holy Land Conservation Fund

Chairman, International Israel Economic Conference, Jerusalem/U.S.
Section, 1967–1973

Vice President, Israel Histadrut Campaign

Member, Board of Governors, Jewish Agency, Inc. President, Jewish
Committee for Personal Service

Chairman, State of Israel Bond Committee, Greater Los Angeles Area

International Chairman, Member of Board of Directors,
Tel Aviv University

Adrea Carter in 2002.

Epilogue
Adrea Carter, 1910–2006

As this book neared completion, my beloved mother, Adrea Carter, passed away, on July 24, 2006, at age ninety-six. It seemed appropriate to acknowledge her life separate and apart from that of her husband, in commemoration of the long, dignified, joyous, creative, and philanthropic life that she also led.

My mother could be the subject of her own book—she had enough wisdom, grace, and savvy not just to play the part of Mrs. Victor M. Carter, a role she filled with delight, but also to be the star of her own life. My mother was vital to my father's success, as we have seen. The certainty that she provided him—of a happy and safe home—allowed him to create the unparalleled success about which you have read in this book. That success, in turn, enabled my mother to follow her own dreams and to contribute to her family and her community in remarkable ways.

My father might have been the fundraiser and organizer in the family, but my mother carved out philanthropic and civic areas of responsibility of her own. She became the president of the Hamburger Home for Girls, later known as Aviva Center, a residence for young girls whose parents were no longer with them. As the president of that organization, she raised considerable funds and was responsible for the well-being of many, many young women. My mother learned organizational and fundraising techniques from the master, and my father certainly helped her find her way in the worlds of philanthropy and community service, but the Hamburger Home was her own project and responsibility.

Similarly, as president of the Music Commission for Los Angeles, my mother was involved for decades with the expansion of cultural life in the city. With my father's encouragement, she helped to increase the visibility of the L.A. Philharmonic, and under her direction, the commission was deeply involved in programming, selecting conductors, and other aspects of the administration and organization of the philharmonic.

As a leading fundraiser for the women's division of the United Jewish Welfare Fund, my mother gave elegant luncheons and participated in high-level fundraising activities for an organization that benefits charitable institutions in Israel and the United States.

.   .

YET THE PHILANTHROPIC and community service side of my mother was just one aspect of her nature, one facet of her remarkable character. She was my mom. She loved to plan wonderful birthday parties, buy cute clothing for me when I was a child, and share with me her love of music, art, and culture. How can I forget how she managed to run our house in the most beautiful way, despite the agony she experienced every day for seventeen years as the mother of a son with muscular dystrophy.

Her parents lived next door to us, and her sister next door to them, creating a supportive compound as my mother took care of Bobby. She had a lot to contend with, and she handled everything without complaining, with grace and dignity, and with a smile. She always had the ability to get dressed, go out with my father, with me, or with both of us, and have a wonderful time. She loved to go to movies, concerts, and the theater, but she also loved to be with her family.

After her passing, I found her diary for 1928, a, simple, elegant leather-bound notebook that contained her excited recordings of the events of her first year of marriage. For me the most charming entry was "We ran away and eloped to Tijuana today." I think of her as she was then, a young "flapper," beautiful, talented, deeply in love, the world at her feet, in these years prior to the Depression and Bobby's birth and illness.

Her diary entries for 1928 are delightful and poignant. It seems as though the newlyweds went out every night, or close to it. There wasn't a movie they didn't see, and if they enjoyed it, they would see it again and again. Her diary spoke of seeing the movie *Wings*, the first film ever to win Best Picture at the Oscars. "We saw Ramon Navarro," another entry read. And then, movingly, "I love him so much—I wish he wouldn't work so hard." And on another day, "We found out we were pregnant today—we're such a happy family!"

My mother maintained that spirit of enthusiasm and *joie de vivre* over a lifespan that fell only a few years shy of a century. Her life is the best advertisement for joyousness, activity, family, contribution, and philanthropy that one could imagine. As Rabbi Jacob Pressman said in his eulogy of her, which follows, she was a queen in this life, and her regal nature is sorely missed. She was a woman with great qualities, and now her spirit moves on to another plane.

Mystical Judaism believes in the reincarnation of souls, and I can only believe that my parents have been reunited, their spirits joyfully roaming the universe, preparing for their next lives on this terrestrial plane. My parents were never cynics, despite the grim headlines and tragedies of the twentieth century, a period that nearly matched their own lifespans. They had faith in the self-correcting nature of mankind, and believed, no matter what negative experience came their way or the world's way, that this, too, would pass.

I know that my own immediate sense of grief over losing my mother will pass, to be replaced by an even deeper appreciation of who she was, how she lived, and the radiant spirit of optimism and joy that defined her. How appropriate, therefore, that a book about my father ends with a tribute to the woman who brought out the best in him, and in me.

EULOGY FOR ADREA ZUCKER CARTER

JULY 26, 2006   RABBI JACOB PRESSMAN

ADREA CARTER

Born: November 10, 1910   Mt. Sinai Memorial Park
Died: July 24, 2006   Rabbi Jacob Pressman

Dear Friends:

FOR MANY YEARS IN OUR COMMUNITY we had a Jewish Camelot, presided over by our king and queen, Victor and Adrea Carter. Those times were very much like these, when the future of the Jewish people was threatened by enemies round about. The Carter home became the seat of operations for the mobilizing of the support of the Jewish community and any others who were sympathetic. Victor was either the founder, or the president, or the prime benefactor of virtually every Israeli, humanitarian, or economic public venture in this city and beyond. But he was not alone. By his side, gracious hostess to presidents and prime ministers of many lands, was his beautiful, worldly partner in life, Adrea. I maintain, without fear of contradiction, that Victor would not have been the great man he became had he not had a woman of the grace and stature in her own right like Adrea. It is realistic to say that they created each other, and together gave us a rare time, a Camelot all our own.

Adrea was born in Irvington, New Jersey, to Anne and Morris Zucker, and, fortunately for us, they moved here when she was only two. Here she was raised and schooled, and here something *beshert*, preordained, happened when she was only 17. It seems that a young man named Victor worked in a hardware store with his father, Mark Carter. One day, a customer, Morris Zucker, came into the store, and was extremely impressed with the knowledgeable, hard-working, personable young man behind the counter. Morris invited Victor and his mother Fanya to the Zucker home, to discuss the possibility of building a new house for the Carters.

That visit was the occasion when Victor and Adrea first met. Victor, who already was accustomed to decision-making, and knew a good thing when he saw it, was smitten by Adrea. He believed he was seeing the most beautiful girl in the world, a belief he held all the days of his life. Five days later they were married. Did anybody say it wouldn't last? Maybe, but it lasted for 75 years of an incredible story of love and compatibility and mutual respect. Adrea developed into the gracious, stylish queen of our local society, who kept pace with her meteoric husband, the king.

. .

I KNOW THERE ARE PEOPLE HERE who are remembering acts of kindness and consideration Adrea performed for them as if it were second nature. My wife, Margie, reminded me of the time when Adrea and Victor were making one of their many trips to Israel. In advance, Adrea, knowing our daughter Judy had made Aiiyah, called Margie and asked if there was anything Judy needed, anything they could carry over for her. I remember Adrea welcoming us to their beautiful penthouse atop Hotel Moriah in Jerusalem, filled with breathtaking art, and affording an even more breathtaking, 360-degree panoramic view of the entire Jerusalem area. I invite you to recall times of peace and joy you spent with them wherever they were. They are what you must remember long after this time of grief and bereavement is past, positive memories of good times with Adrea, good times which were not achieved without great challenges they had to overcome.

I marvel when I think of what that young couple sustained after their marriage in 1929: the immediate crash of the market; the onset of the Great Depression; the death of Victor's beloved mother Fanya Carter; the rumblings of the oncoming Holocaust of the Jews by Hitler; the tragic, untimely loss of their one son, Bobby, at the age of 17, victim of muscular dystrophy. These hardships were counterbalanced for them with the birth of their second child, Fanya.

Adrea and Fanya bonded early in life, not merely as mother and daughter, but as best friends, a deep and abiding mutual love and admiration society which lasted until Adrea's last breath. Adrea's mother, Anne, was a teacher of piano, and taught Adrea. Adrea, in turn, loved to play the piano with Fanya; to dance together with her like two girlfriends, to respect each other as mature women, to console each other when Victor died two years ago, and then to have roles reversed when Fanya nurtured her mother as she declined and drifted slowly out of this world bathed in love.

Saturday afternoon we gathered at Adrea's bedside where she lay in her own home, with the hospice caretaker nearby. I held her hand with one of mine, and Fanya's hand with the other, and as I began to chant the *Shema Yisrael* I heard Fanya

Adrea's parents, Anne and Morris Zucker.

chanting the words with me. I must believe that somehow Adrea heard her daughter's voice singing Israel's ancient watchword as the last sound she heard on this earth. The next day, Sunday, was Fanya's birthday. Adrea was dying. But, in that strange way that little miracles happen, Adrea held on so as not to darken that happy day for Fanya, held on until that day ended at midnight, Sunday. Then, one hour and twenty minutes later, she passed away, witnesses say, with a smile on her face.

. .

A CAMELOT ERA HAS COME TO AN END. The Queen is going to lie eternally beside her King, and we are left to thank God for the years she has had and for the peace and rest which are now hers.

May her soul be bound up in the bond of eternal life.

Adrea Carter's maternal grandparents, Sam and Mary Orbach, and children.

Sam and Mary Orbach in Manhattan in 1899.

Index

Page numbers in **boldface**
indicate photographs.

About the Author

Born in Hollywood Hospital, Fanya Carter spent her childhood surrounded by the glamour and excitement of Los Angeles during the years of that city's remarkable growth. She experienced the rich combination of her Jewish and Russian heritage in the home of her parents, Victor M. and Adrea Carter.

As a young woman, Dr. Carter devoted herself to marriage and family, raising three "baby boom"-era children in Encino and Beverly Hills in the years following World War II. While her children were in school, she returned to her own studies, earned her master's degree and doctorate, and developed a thriving practice as a clinical psychologist. She continues to practice psychology today.

With the passing of Victor M. Carter in 2004, Dr. Carter realized a compelling need to write the life story of her amazing father — businessman, philanthropist, and, above all, humanitarian.

Dr. Carter lives in Santa Monica, California, with her husband, retired psychoanalyst Jack Delchamps.

"All the Best!"
THE LIFE OF VICTOR M. CARTER

Editor: JACKIE PELS, Hardscratch Press

Book composition and production: DAVID R. JOHNSON

Proofreader: PETER KUPFER

Printed at INKWORKS PRESS, Berkeley, Calif.   147 INKWORKS

Alkaline pH recycled paper ♲

Bound at CARDOZA-JAMES, San Francisco, Calif.